The Vocabulary of Literature

Teacher Manual

Michael Clay Thompson

Royal Fireworks Press
Unionville, New York

October 2017

Copyright © 2015
Royal Fireworks Publishing Company, Inc.
All Rights Reserved. All Copying Prohibited.
Royal Fireworks Publishing Company
41 First Avenue, P.O. Box 399
Unionville, NY 10988
tel: (845) 726-4444
fax: (845) 726-3824
email: mail@rfwp.com
website: rfwp.com

ISBN
Teacher Manual: 978-0-88092-873-1
Student Book: 978-0-88092-872-4

Publisher: Dr. T.M. Kemnitz
Design and graphics: Michael Clay Thompson
Cover designer: Kerri Ann Ruhl
Editors: Jennifer Ault and Rachel Semlyen

Printed and bound in Unionville, New York, on acid-free paper
using vegetable-based inks at the Royal Fireworks facility.

6o17 ps

About the cover: The cover photographs are front and rear views of Rudyard Kipling's home in East Sussex. Built in the reign of King James I and completed in 1634, the house had not been modified in the years before Kipling first saw it in 1900. He purchased it and lived there from 1902 until his death in 1936. It was here that he wrote some of his most famous work. He and his wife loved the house, and she left it to be maintained as a museum after her death in 1939. It remains as the Kiplings left it. Photographs by Dr. Thomas Milton Kemnitz.

Table of Contents

Reading Is Personal

My hope for this book is that we will explore much of the vocabulary you need for a lifetime of reading. In the long term, the reading you do will determine the strength of your education.

I would like to talk about books in personal terms because reading is one of the most personal experiences in life. In most cases, you read by yourself, and the bulk of the reading you do is not assigned or graded. Usually, no one knows what you are reading or even that you are reading. It is your business. Even though you will love many of the great books you read as part of your school experience, your best reading is done outside of school or after you have graduated, and you choose your books yourself. School can help you get started and give you a good reading foundation, but school years are of short duration (though it does not seem so at the time), and you will only do a small fraction of your great reading during those years. Even during my school years in elementary school and beyond, I was already reading — both for fun and for information — far beyond anything assigned to me, and books were an important part of my personal life.

Books have been my road to adventure and to understanding things about the world and about myself that I would never have known without them. Books have allowed me to surround myself with writers of genius and extraordinary imagination, many of whom died centuries before I was born and whose words still take me to their centuries for long visits. Their books have nourished my spirit with amazing vocabulary that I never hear otherwise, and they have filled my mind with sentences that are perfect works of thought. They have challenged my assumptions, given me heroes to admire, and warned me of cruel villains. I have learned, through the safety of a book, the great wrongs that human beings can do to one another, and I have learned about people, fictional and historical, who care profoundly about others. These experiences have been personal.

I have stood on the soaked deck in a rising sea, the white foam flying from the waves and the wind whipping my face, and searched the western horizon for Treasure Island. I have hidden in a barrel in the rancid hold and heard the scoundrel pirates whisper my name in malicious hisses. I heard them plot my death. I have believed the devious lies of that sweet-tongued villain, Long John Silver. I thought quickly and showed them all.

I have been the horrid, sewed-up creation of Dr. Victor Frankenstein. My monster stitches sore and stinging, I have crept in the cold snow toward a cabin of people, a sweet family, and longed to be their friend, and trudged through the frozen drifts to gather firewood to keep them warm when they never knew my face. And if they had seen my face and my monstrous form wrapped in rags, they would have fled screaming into the night. They never knew what kind soul brought them the good firewood. I did it.

I have been a whiskery water rat, rowing my small boat down the willowy river to visit my friend, the blinky mole, and we have had such a breakfast by the fire in his cozy burrow. We have visited our eccentric friend, Toad of Toad Hall, and have seen him speed away in his motorcar, swerving uncontrollably and leaving billows of dust in the road behind him. Oblivious to everything but himself, he hardly knew we were there, so astonished was he at his own dreams of adventure. We stuck by him anyway.

I have stood in a polite drawing room with Miss Elizabeth Bennett and heard her make the most profound observations about the posturing and hypocrisy around her. I have winced at the sharp edge of her wit. I have seen her reject the hand of the richest man in the land out of loyalty to her sister. I have seen her expostulate with her father to exercise more control of her wild younger sister, only to have her wisdom rejected, tragically. Elizabeth never knew I was there.

I have designed and built a gleaming, whirring time machine, and I have ridden it through a swirl of light and glory far into the distant future, where the sun was enormous and red, like a dying throb, and the myriad species of the earth were reduced to grotesque crabs scraping across the muddy shore of a lifeless sea, and farther down the gray shore some amorphous flappy thing gave me chills. I have been poked and prodded by hideous, ashen Morlocks, and I swung my flaming torch to keep them back. Even my best friends never believed me when I told them—nay, I *showed* them—what I had accomplished. Only I know what happened to me.

I have been a huge house dog, the beloved pet of my family, kidnapped and caged and chained and taken to the frozen North, where the wild winds howl and the rivers freeze and the whipped huskies drag the sleds across the barren wastes of snow. I have heard the snap of the whip and the yelps of the dogs. I have heard the long, long howls of my wild cousins, the merciless wolves, and have stared at the white moon and howled too, and howled again. I have become one with my howl, my call. I have fought with great, furious dogs, and have dodged their snapping fangs, and have taught them the red lesson they deserved. They never challenged me again. In the lonely northland, I had one friend, John Thornton, but he is gone now, and it hurts me to think of him.

I have shipped aboard a reeking whaler, the *Pequod*, and set sail for the South Seas, and have traded jokes with my one true friend, the tattooed cannibal Queequeg—a taciturn, honest man—and have seen the eyes of mad Ahab, the crazed monomaniac whose only dream in life was the death of a hated whale, the white whale Moby Dick. I watched as that tormented whale turned and destroyed our ship and pulled everything under the sea, pulled even Ahab under the sea, and I alone survived. I tell the tale.

I have gone with young Jane Eyre as she took a job as a governess, only to come under the spell of her rich employer, the eccentric Mr. Rochester, and I have seen her stand her ground and speak her mind and assert her true individuality even in the face of the harshest consequences. I have seen her courage and wanted to have courage as strong as hers. I have seen her face deceit and betrayal and respond with loyalty and love.

I have been a spirited lad in rural England, raised by my strict sister and her gentle husband Joe. We were poor, and we had little education, and we scraped by. One day we heard that a murderous escaped convict was on the prowl in the moor near our house, and crossing the moor I encountered him, to my terror. Disheveled and muddy, he told me to get him wittles (victuals, food) and a file, which I did, in fear for my life. He was soon captured. Years afterward a strange man came to our house and told me that I had great expectations and that from an anonymous benefactor I would inherit a fortune and become a gentleman. Little did I know that my mysterious benefactor was the pitiful escaped convict, Magwitch, who had made a great fortune in the New World and who never forgot my kindness to him.

I have floated down the great river on a raft with my pal Jim, an escaped slave, and have learned that true friendship demands true freedom, and have been fast friends in the face of the worst hatreds of mean-souled society, and have drifted down the river in the great black star-night, and have seen the steamboat chugging along in the dark, and have watched the sparks of the chimneys rain down on the water. I will never forget that.

I have flown up into the sky to Neverland, somewhere beyond the third star on the right, where I would never grow up, and have known the lost boys, and have heard the ticking of the cranky crocodile, and have clashed swords with that crooked Hook and his cruel pirate crew—those fools. They never were smart enough to defeat me. I have been the loyal ally of Tiger Lily, and have fought brave battles at her side, and then swapped sides and played the battles again, to be fair.

I have done all of these things and more. I am the one. Through books I have traveled the world. I have lived through the centuries. I have seen the past. In Nemo's *Nautilus*, I have descended to the silent deep. I have waltzed in great ballrooms, and I have scaled great mountain faces. I have snuck through the woods, trying to reach the fort alive. It was not easy.

In the long summer nights, I have opened a new book, and smelled the new paper and the ink, and have settled down with a cold drink of water, and begun the great story, carefully, without bending the pages back or breaking the spine of the book. I have read long into the night, as the words fell into my mind and the waves fell onto the shore outside my window, or as the palm fronds clickered outside my window screen, or as the taxis honked somewhere in the city. Sometimes in the distance I could hear a train, and I would look up from the South Pacific or the dark forest, but then I would look back down. I have enjoyed those night sounds, but they did not pull me out of the book. Eventually the sun would peek up over the sea or the city, or the ocean breeze would come in my window and blow the curtain, and a bird would exclaim, and I would realize that I should get some sleep, but I was careful to put a bookmark on my page so that I could go right back to that same moment in the story.

I did not want to miss a thing.

I have done all of these things through the creative spell of books. I have done them through the creative genius of writers such as Jane Austen, and Charles Dickens, and Jack London, and Charlotte Brontë, and I have immersed myself in nonfiction classics such as the great *Narrative* of Frederick Douglass and Rachel Carson's *Silent Spring*.

Books, and the Alternative

Today, television and films compete for our attention, but there is nothing like a book. Books are not like films, which never stop to talk to you. Films push forward irrevocably at their own pell-mell pace that is visual rather than thoughtful. The film keeps moving, like a talker who will not let you get a word in edgewise. If you get distracted, the film moves on anyway. When you read a book, you have time to think. You can stop when you want to and read a part of it again. The book stops with you. It is comfortable. You can go back to listen to a conversation more carefully. You can stay in your favorite parts and only leave when you are ready. It is up to you.

When you read a book, you can copy out your favorite passages onto cards and pin them to your wall.

Films are noisy, full of chatter and background music and sound effects. Films have gunshots and explosions and shouting and screaming and the screech of tires. Books are quiet and peaceful, and you can imagine the sounds they describe for yourself. Books do not have background music; instead, they have poetic effects woven into their words.

A film of a book might last ninety minutes, but the book that the film skims might last days, giving you time to know the characters deeply and become friends with them. The book shows you things about the characters that the film leaves out. Notice that most great books are long. They last for hundreds of pages. You become involved in the book, but unlike a film that will end within the hour, the fun of a book continues, and you wish it would never end. Long books teach you to hold your attention, which is one of life's best lessons.

Most films were made within the last one hundred years. Many great books are not only works of art but are also artifacts; they were written in the nineteenth century or the eighteenth century, and you can read them in their pure form, without a modernizing translation that robs them of their authenticity and substance. An eighteenth-century book was actually written by an eighteenth-century person. You might have to read two or three books from an earlier century to get the hang of it, but that too is part of the fun.

Books are the perfect place to learn words. In a film you do not quite hear a word that passes too fast. It is a transient blur. You are not sure what the character said, how it was pronounced, or how it was spelled, and in a split second it is gone forever. You cannot think about the word because immediately there are new words to hear, and your attention shifts to those. The film's words whirl by like horses on a merry-go-round. Nothing holds still. In a book you can see the words steady on the page, and look at how they are spelled, and think about how they are pronounced. You can pause to look up a word. You can do it your way.

In a book you can also see the punctuation, and notice the commas, and stop when the periods say so. Punctuation is inaudible. Films do not show punctuation.

In a film the best words of the book might be replaced by modern or simple words, but in the book you enjoy the full fun of the greatest storytelling vocabulary of literature, and you get to know the words, and you see them again ten pages later, and fourteen pages after that. As you read, you absorb the best words of the century in which the book was written, and as I already have indicated, after you read a few books from that century, you fit in, and you are comfortable, and you can then read anything from that century and have such fun, as though you had lived in that time. Books preserve the life of their centuries for all time. If you want to know about a previous century, read a book about that century written during that century by a person who lived in that century.

Two different films of the same book will show two different visions, two different interpretations. The book is always the same. It is the author's exact, original story.

And the more books you read, the more you understand, and the more you enjoy, and the more stories you absorb to help you through the rough spots of life. You develop of a sense of what Odysseus would do, or what Elizabeth Bennet would say, or how Queequeg would come to your side. You find yourself influenced by one character, and similar to another, and memorizing the exact words of another. Bit by bit, the stories become part of you.

And one book leads to another. You read a book by Jack London, and you enjoy it so much that you want to read another written by him. I have sometimes read an author's complete works. As you read books by the same author, you get to know the author's style and point of view. You become familiar with Ernest Hemingway's succinct, concrete writing and his view of individuals trying to face life with courage. You come to understand Charles Dickens's sympathy for people who have little and for their dignity and importance, even as they are poor and humble. You learn Jane Austen's regard for women who stand their ground and who do not permit their equality to be dismissed.

There is a saying among book beginners that goes, "I've already read that." But true readers are rereaders. Real readers know that it takes a number of readings to absorb a book. Real readers love to reread their favorite books. Real readers do not think, "I've already read that." To have already read a great book is a necessary step in the even better reading that one now begins. You read, and before you know it, you are going to your shelf to find that book again, to read the book again because it is now one of your favorites, with your favorite characters saying your favorite things. I may have read Shakespeare's *Hamlet* fifty times, but I have not finished reading it. I am never finished. I never throw my books away or give them away. I always try to buy hardback books because they are not disposable to me. I read them, and they become part of my life, and they take their place in my collection. They are like songs that we want to hear again whenever we wish.

Books: education means books. There is no substitute for books. More than anything else, it is the reading and rereading of books that educates us. Merely going to school, if the experience does not lead us into a world of books, does not ensure that we become educated. And the necessary experience with books is essentially personal; no school can possibly assign the amount of reading that true education demands. Schools help us begin, but schools only train us to read. School reading points the way. We use that brief foundation to launch ourselves into a life of reading.

We sometimes hear the phrase "the life of the mind." The main gate to the life of the mind is a stack of books. Through books, you have access to the great ideas in intellectual history, to the great movements of armies and civilizations, to the great discoveries of science, to the lives of the heroes, to the ideas of the philosophers, to the suffering of the martyrs, to the great characters and themes in literature. Books are the common language that unites thinking people the world over, and the more you read, the more you can enjoy both your own ideas and the ideas of others across the world and through the centuries.

In this book you will find a strong selection of classic words—the power words that I identified in my research as critical to an enjoyment of the classics of British and American literature. Each lesson presents ten new classic words, and each lesson also contains ten classic words brought forward from *Caesar's English I* and *Caesar's English II*, so students who studied those texts will find those words strengthened, and students who did not study those texts will learn them now. Each chapter contains famous examples and creative readings that will help you internalize the classic words. In all, this collection of words will pave your path into great English literature. Read with spirit, believe in the words, make it your intention to learn them permanently, and look forward to the wonderful literature that you will enjoy.

JACK
LONDON

Classic Words – Lesson I

Ten New Words

latter: the second

dejected: in low spirits

despondent: disheartened

rebuke: a sharp criticism

writhe: twist, squirm

aloof: unfriendly

dissipate: disperse

portent: an omen

phenomenon: an unusual occurrence

resolute: determined

Ten Review Words

Caesar's English I

countenance: facial expression

profound: deep

manifest: obvious

prodigious: huge

languor: weakness

Caesar's English II

placate: to appease

derision: ridicule

vivacious: full of life

procure: to acquire

retort: a quick, clever reply

latter: adj., LATT-ur, rhymes with *bladder*

The adjective **latter** means the second item of two. If there are more than two items, we simply refer to the "last mentioned." In *The Red Badge of Courage*, Stephen Crane wrote that "The latter felt immensely superior to his friend." In Emily Brontë's *Wuthering Heights*, we read that "She tossed a cushion under his head, and offered him some water; he rejected the latter, and tossed uneasily on the former."

dejected: adj., de-JECK-ted, rhymes with *collected*

The adjective **dejected** means sad or depressed, as the stems *de* (down) and *ject* (throw) suggest: thrown down, emotionally. The noun form is *dejection*. In James M. Barrie's *Peter Pan*, we read that "Hook was profoundly dejected." In Sir Walter Scott's *Ivanhoe*, Scott noted that "Her demeanour was serious, but not dejected."

despondent: adj., de-SPON-dent, rhymes with *correspondent*

The adjective **despondent** (the noun forms are *despondence, despond,* or *despondency*) means profoundly disheartened, dispirited from loss of hope. In Kenneth Grahame's *The Wind in the Willows*, we read that "He's always rather low and despondent when he's wanting his victuals." Victuals are food. In *Gulliver's Travels*, Jonathan Swift wrote that "I found myself so listless and desponding that I had not the heart to rise."

rebuke: n. or v., re-BYOOK, rhymes with *fluke*

The noun **rebuke** indicates a sharp reprimand, a severe criticism. We also use *rebuke* as a verb. In Charles Dickens's *A Tale of Two Cities*, we read that "Loud acclamations hailed this rebuke." In William Makepeace Thackeray's *Vanity Fair*, "That gentleman rose up with an oath and rebuked Rawdon for his language."

writhe: v., RYTHE, rhymes with *scythe*

The verb **writhe** means to twist or to squirm, to contort the body. In Thomas Hardy's *Jude the Obscure*, we read that "Sue writhed under the hard and direct questioning." In Mary Shelley's *Frankenstein*, the pitiful monster laments, "I now writhed under the miserable pain of a wound."

aloof: adj., ah-LOOF, rhymes with *roof*

The adjective **aloof** means distant, unfriendly, cool. It is often used with *stand*; we stand aloof, either emotionally or physically. In Jane Austen's *Pride and Prejudice*, "They stood a little aloof while he was talking to their niece." James M. Barrie, in *Peter Pan*, wrote, "Ever a dark and solitary enigma, he stood aloof from his followers."

dissipate: v., DISS-ih-pate, rhymes with *anticipate*

The verb **dissipate** means to disperse, to scatter, to break up, to disappear. The noun *dissipation* usually refers to an undisciplined life of luxury or pleasure. In Mary Shelley's *Frankenstein*, we read that "Presently a breeze dissipated the cloud, and I descended upon the glacier." In *Walden*, Henry David Thoreau wrote that "The student may read Homer or Aeschylus in the Greek without danger of dissipation or luxuriousness."

portent: n., POR-tent, rhymes with *important*

The noun **portent** means an omen, a warning sign. The adjective form is *portentous*. In *Lord Jim*, Joseph Conrad wrote that "They had him, but it was like getting hold of an apparition, a wraith, a portent." In Herman Melville's *Moby Dick*, we read that "Such a portentous and mysterious monster roused all my curiosity."

phenomenon: n., feh-NOH-me-non, rhymes with *Parthenon*

The singular noun **phenomenon** refers to a fact or situation that may not be fully understood. Important: The plural is *phenomena*: a phenomenon, some phenomena. In *The Yearling*, Marjorie Kinnan Rawlings wrote that "The sinkhole was a phenomenon common to the Florida limestone regions." In Henry David Thoreau's *Walden,* we read that "Few phenomena gave me more delight."

resolute: adj., REH-zo-loot, rhymes with *salute*

The adjective **resolute** means determined or firm, usually in an admirable sense. The opposite is *irresolute*. In Bram Stoker's *Dracula*, we read that "He was never so resolute, never so strong, never so full of volcanic energy, as at present."

Jack London

The ability to read academic nonfiction is one of the most important elements of academic success. For practice, here is a short nonfiction essay that contains many of the classic words of this lesson.

A writer of rugged countenance and prodigious talent, Jack London was the author of *White Fang*, *The Call of the Wild*, *The Sea Wolf*, and other stories that have become classics of American literature.

Born in San Francisco in 1876, London knew from an early age that he wanted to be a writer, but he spent years struggling despondently from one low-paying job to another. He worked at a cannery, was an oyster-pirate, worked on the California Fish Patrol, was a sailor, and was even a hobo—in 1894 the dejected London was incarcerated for thirty days for vagrancy. Eventually he returned home, graduated from Oakland High School, and was admitted to the University of California at Berkeley, but he dropped out because he did not have enough money to pay his university bills. London was a great reader, and in his later years he procured a personal library of more than 15,000 books.

In 1897 London went to the Alaskan Klondike, resolutely chasing a dream of gold, but he suffered under the cruel conditions and developed scurvy. His experiences left him with a profound social conscience, and he began to weave his experiences into vivacious stories that depicted the struggle for existence amid the cruel phenomena of wild nature, where the weak and languorous are dominated by the strong. He wrote his first major novel, *The Call of the Wild*, which is set in the Yukon, in 1903. *The Call of the Wild* has never been out of print since it was first published, and it has now been translated into nearly fifty languages.

All authors experience sharp critical reviews, even derision, and London was no different. Some have questioned his manifest emphasis on violence, and others have rebuked him for ethnocentric prejudice. It is not unusual for writers to draw on other sources for ideas, but some critics feel that London went beyond normal influence and plagiarized other authors' work—a charge he rejected.

Since London's death in 1916 at the age of only forty, his fame as a novelist has not dissipated. His major titles are part of the canon of world literature, and they continue to be read and discussed.

Q: What interests you most about Jack London's life? What would you like to read more about?

Jack London

Michael Clay Thompson

Jack London stumbled down the dock.
Dejection hurt his heart.   n.
An omen had appeared, a flock,
a portent, dark, a start   n.

of some phenomenon. He looked   n.
into the writhing wind,   adj.
his canvas backpack crammed with books,
and dreamed of spinning

tales of cold, despondent worlds,   adj.
of snow, prodigious storms,   adj.
and brutes, rebukes, and whirling   n.
mists with dissipating forms   adj.

of circling wolves. A languor filled   n.
his listless limbs. He stowed
his stuff aboard the ship. He'd build
these grimy details into code,

into his art of words, aloof,   adj.
of Nature's fallen fools,
of ice and knives, and fang and tooth,
and countenances cruel.   n.

He well perceived the portent's truth: n.
the resolute survive.   n.
The weak succumb to fang and tooth,
the strong prevail—alive.

Classic Words Challenge

In each case below, one of the choices was the word used by the author. Your challenge is to guess which word the author used. This is not a test; it is a game because more than one word choice may work perfectly well. Use your sensitivity and intuition to guess which word the author used. You may need a dictionary.

1. From Stephen Crane's *The Red Badge of Courage*

   He was _______ and sullen, and threw shifting glances about him.
   a. aloof
   b. despondent
   c. resolute
   d. profound

2. From H.G. Wells's *The War of the Worlds*

   All day and all night we sat face to face, I weary but __________.
   a. aloof
   b. dejected
   c. despondent
   d. resolute

3. From Johann David Wyss's *The Swiss Family Robinson*

   We were attracted by a most curious __________.
   a. phenomenon
   b. rebuke
   c. portent
   d. countenance

4. From James M. Barrie's *Peter Pan*

   Ever a dark and solitary enigma, he stood _______ from his followers.
   a. dejected
   b. despondent
   c. aloof
   d. manifest

Classic Grammar • Parts of Speech

Every vocabulary word is a part of speech, and every sentence is made of vocabulary. To use vocabulary correctly, we must use it grammatically. Many words can be used in several ways. The word *run*, for example, can be a verb, as in *We run every day*; it also can be a noun: *We had a good run.*

In the sentences below, you will find our classic vocabulary words, but they may be present as a different part of speech. In other words, you may see a classic adjective we know but in its adverb form or noun form. Think flexibly. On the lines below sentences three through seven, write the part of speech of each word. If you need to review the eight parts of speech, do that first.

1. He   tramped   **despondently**   up   and   down   the   region. (Twain)

   pron.   v.   adv.   prep.   conj.   prep.   adj.   n.

____

2. The   **aloofness**...existed   when   we   first   met   in   Naples.... (James Watson)

   adj.   n.   v.   conj. pron. adv.   v. prep.   n.

____

3. The   lama   took   snuff   from   a   **portentous**   wooden   snuff-gourd. (Kipling)

   adj.   n.   v.   n.   prep. adj.   adj.   adj.   n.

____

4. Hook   was   profoundly   **dejected**. (Barrie)

    n.   v.   adv.   adj.

____

5. On   they   trudged   and   **writhed**   and   surged. (W.E.B. Du Bois)

   adv. pron.   v.   conj.   v.   conj.   v.

____

6. There   was   no   voice   of   **rebuke**. (Twain)

   adv.   v.   adj.   n.   prep.   n.

____

7. My   fear   was   instantly   **dissipated**. (M. Shelley)

   adj.   n.   v.   adv.   v.   (*was dissipated* is the passive voice verb)

____

Classic Word Muddles

In most of the sentences below, one of the classic words is misused, which means that it is a part of speech error. Remember, parts of speech are the instructions for correct vocabulary usage. Can you explain the vocabulary/grammar errors? Some of the sentences contain no errors.

1. When Austen saw the **writhe**, she became more resolute.   not a n.
2. His dejection increased, and he made a **countenance** face.   not an adj.
3. The **rebuke** remark made Hawthorne stand aloof.   not an adj.
4. The latter remark caused **portent** alarm.   not an adj.
5. The disturbing portent left London **despondent**.   correct
6. Thoreau thought about a prodigious **phenomena**.   phenomenon
7. Crane's dejected countenance made his sadness **manifest**.   correct
8. Dickinson's sleepy languor gave her a manifest **aloof**.   not a n.
9. Frost chose the latter path, and his dejection **dissipated**.   correct
10. The comment stung, and he made a **writhe** face.   not an adj.

Classic Centuries: *dejected*

Below are examples of how *dejected* has been used through the centuries. Which is your favorite?

1952   Bernard Malamud, *The Natural*
"The New York Yankees grew more dejected."

1904   James M. Barrie, *Peter Pan*
"He was roused from this dejection by Smee's eager voice."

1895   Stephen Crane, *The Red Badge of Courage*
"Their smudged countenances now expressed a profound dejection."

1816   Jane Austen, *Emma*
"His dejection was most evident."

1726   Jonathan Swift, *Gulliver's Travels*
"They all appeared with dejected looks, and in the meanest habit."

1667   John Milton, *Paradise Lost*
"Of sorrow and dejection and despair...."

1601   William Shakespeare, *Hamlet*
"Nor the dejected 'havior of the visage."

An Impression, Influenced by Jack London's *The Sea Wolf*

In the story below, some of the classic words are used well, but others are not. Sometimes it is the meaning that is wrong, and other times it is the grammar/usage. Please circle the classic words that are not used correctly.

The scarred old captain clanked across the wooden deck of the schooner, muttering sharp rebukes at his crew. His usual cheerful **dejection** was gone, and he seemed to writhe in fury at his failure to find the pirates that had attacked his ship during the last voyage. He might have been negligent, or he might have been tricked; he preferred the latter explanation. But now he was in no mood for reflection. Aloof and glowering, he stomped past the nervous crew.

In fact, he was in no mood for hesitation; he was furious, energetic, and **languorous**, and he was resolute about catching the pirates. He would allow no retort. He knew that it might take a **phenomenon** event to reveal where they were hiding, and he knew that the answer might be hidden and **manifest**. The situation could be a **profound**.

He remembered the days of his youth, when he had been so hopeful and **despondent**, but those hopes had rapidly dissipated as a series of disturbing portents had proven true. Instead of realizing his dreams, he had suffered under years of **prodigious**, and he knew that now it was too late for him to recover. His only hope was to find the pirates and exact his revenge. Nothing could placate him.

Purple and gray clouds began to amass on the southern horizon, and he knew that a prodigious storm was gathering and **dissipating**. Flocks of birds were flying north high over the mast quickly, as though they were frightened. A swooping seagull dropped a snake from the sky, and it landed on the salty deck, writhing and hissing, and he knew that this was a portent of danger, a disturbing **phenomena**. Far at sea, you had to watch the weather closely. He barked out a command to set the course for north-northwest.

On a small island far to the west, the pirates could just see the captain's sails on the horizon like a white speck of foam on the crest of a wave, and they knew that he was sailing away from them, and they laughed in **dejection**.

Classic Words Character

Let us use some of the words that we are learning. Pretend that you are writing a novel, and write a short description of a character, using some of the words in this lesson. Here is an example:

> Madeline's countenance was disturbed. The rebuke from her mother had left her writhing with disappointment, and now she felt the sting of the derision in her mother's words. She knew that the pain of hurt feelings would eventually dissipate, and her mother might even come to her room and try to placate her resentment, but for now, all she wanted to do was sit in a corner and think of a sharp retort.

Classic Words Place

Now write a short description of a place, a landscape, or a scene, using some of the words in this lesson. Here is an example:

> During the storm, the birch trees had writhed in profound submission to the wind, and the dark clouds had frowned their derisive countenances down upon the valley. The storm was a massive phenomenon, somehow aloof from humanity and yet resolute in bringing life-giving water to the fields. Now, the first hint of vivacious sun began to break through the clouds, and the thunder began to dissipate, but only slowly.

Classic Words Invention

Finally, write a short description of something or someone that you imagine, using some of the words in this lesson. Here is an example:

> Freedom is a profound idea. Life without freedom is a kind of despondence, a prodigious suppression of creativity and individuality, but freedom is also a challenging phenomenon because with freedom we become responsible for rising above languor and accomplishing something meaningful in our lives.

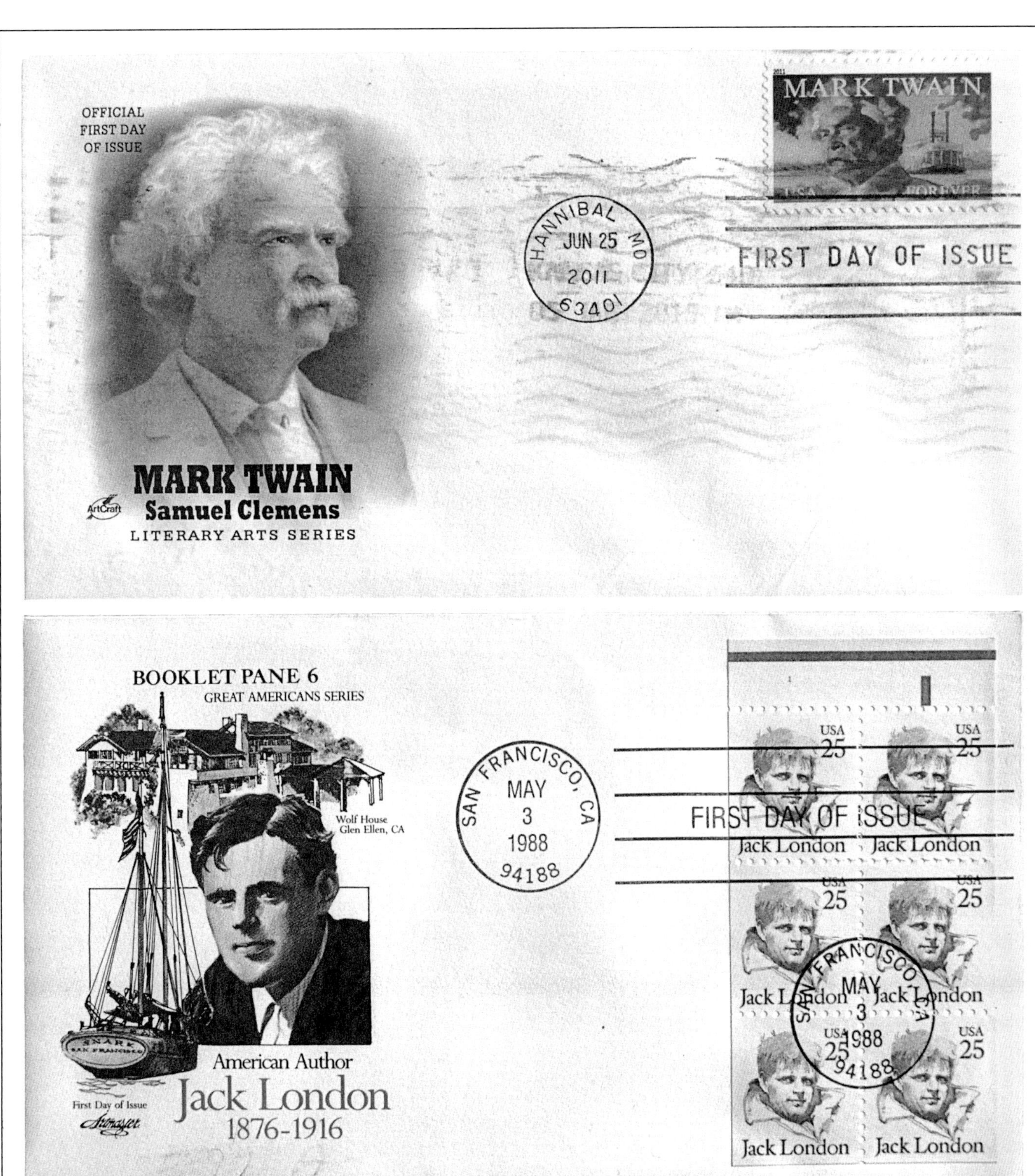

THE UNITED STATES HONORS SOME OF ITS FAVORITE AUTHORS.

JANE AUSTEN

Classic Words – Lesson II

Ten New Words

fain: pleased

entreat: ask earnestly

billow: a wave

reprove: to reprimand

plaintive: mournful

myriad: countless

fervor: passion

conjure: summon

abashed: embarrassed

conjecture: a guess

Ten Review Words

Caesar's English I

melancholy: sadness

serene: calm

amiable: friendly

singular: unique

perplex: confuse

Caesar's English II

audible: able to be heard

benevolent: charitable

somber: gloomy

prostrate: lying flat

profuse: abundant

fain: adj. or adv., FAYNE, rhymes with *rain*

As an adjective or an adverb, **fain** means pleased, gladly. In *Hard Times*, Charles Dickens wrote that "She was fain to take up the note again." In Daniel Defoe's *Robinson Crusoe*, we read, "I would fain have stewed it and made some broth, but had no pot." In Charlotte Brontë's *Jane Eyre*, Jane says, "I would fain exercise some better faculty than that of fierce speaking."

entreat: v., en-TREET, rhymes with *sheet*

The verb **entreat** means to ask earnestly or anxiously. The noun form is *entreaty*. Jane Austen wrote in *Emma* that "now she was too ill to trifle, and must entreat him to set off for Enscombe without delay." In William Shakespeare's *Julius Caesar*, we read, "I do entreat that we may sup together."

billow: n., BILL-oh, rhymes with *pillow*

The noun **billow** refers either to a large wave such as an ocean wave or to any great undulating mass. In *The Swiss Family Robinson*, Johann David Wyss described "the sea, which came in raging billows to meet them, lashed to fury by the tempests of wind." In Robert Louis Stevenson's *Treasure Island*, we read that "the billows rose and fell unbroken."

reprove: v., re-PROOVE, rhymes with *groove*

The verb **reprove** means to reprimand, to scold. We use *reproof* as the noun form. In Jane Austen's *Emma*, we read, "You could not give me a greater reproof for the mistake I fell into." In Charles Dickens's *David Copperfield*, we read that "I was soon bitterly reproved for this harshness."

plaintive: adj., PLANE-tive, rhymes with *cursive*

The adjective **plaintive** means sad, mournful. In Mark Twain's *The Prince and the Pauper*, we read that "Tom buried his head among his pillows, murmuring plaintively." Stephen Crane, in *The Red Badge of Courage*, described how "He could hear the tattered man bleating plaintively." In *The Yearling*, Marjorie Kinnan Rawlings wrote that "Gabby sang a plaintive lament of matrimony."

myriad: n. or adj., MIR-ee-add, rhymes with *fad*

The noun or adjective **myriad** means countless or enormous in number. In *Walden*, Henry David Thoreau refers to "The myriads who built the pyramids to be the tombs of the Pharaohs." In *Dracula*, Bram Stoker wrote, "I seemed to become more wakeful, and myriads of horrible fancies began to crowd in upon my mind."

fervor: n., FER-vor, rhymes with *savor*

The noun **fervor** (or *fervour* in the British spelling) refers to intense or passionate feeling about something. The adjective form is *fervent* or *fervid*. In Charles Dickens's *David Copperfield*, we read about a character "who greeted me with such fervor." In Mary Shelley's *Frankenstein*, her monster says, "I continued with unabated fervour to traverse immense deserts."

conjure: v., KON-jur, rhymes with *injure*

To **conjure** is to summon something, to call it forward. It sometimes means to implore or entreat. The noun form is *conjuration,* and a person who conjures is a conjuror. In Mary Shelley's *Frankenstein*, she wrote, "I walked up and down my room hastily and perturbed, while my imagination conjured up a thousand images to torment and sting me." In Charles Dickens's *David Copperfield*, we read that "He solemnly conjured me, I remember, to take warning by his fate."

abashed: adj., ah-BASHT, rhymes with *mashed*

The adjective **abashed** means embarrassed or ashamed. Someone who is unashamed is *unabashed*. We also see the verb form, to abash. In his novel *Kim*, Rudyard Kipling wrote that "The old soldier looked as abashed as a child interrupted in his game of make-believe." In Ralph Ellison's *Invisible Man*, we read, "Then I saw the foolish, abashed expression on Wrestrum's face and relaxed."

conjecture: v. or n., kon-JECK-chure, rhymes with *lecture*

The verb or noun **conjecture** refers to a guess. In Rachel Carson's great book about the dangers of DDT and other pesticides, *Silent Spring*, she wrote, "At present our answers to these questions are for the most part only conjectures." In Joseph Conrad's *Lord Jim*, we read, "My mind floated in a sea of conjectures." In Mary Shelley's *Frankenstein*, we read that "Elizabeth conjectured that he might have returned to the house."

Jane Austen

The ability to read academic nonfiction is one of the most important elements of academic success. For practice, here is a short nonfiction essay that contains many of the classic words of this lesson.

Jane Austen wrote several of the most beloved novels in English literature, including *Pride and Prejudice* and *Emma*. Writing first under the *nom de plume* "A Lady," Austen eventually achieved literary recognition during her lifetime (1775-1817), but that recognition did not translate into independent wealth, as it did for Sir Walter Scott or for Charles Dickens. Jane Austen's circumstances were modest when her father was alive and were reduced after his death when she became dependent on her brother's aid.

Literary scholars appreciated the succinct power of Austen's writing, and a prodigious billow of critical admiration occurred during the middle of the twentieth century. The popularity of her novels has never dissipated, and they are now a phenomenon in English literature.

Austen's novels conjure forth a myriad of English society's foibles and eccentricities, including elegant courtesies, fervent admirations, abashed sisters, sharp rebukes, sanctimonious reproofs, amiable dunces, languid dandies, aloof aristocrats, despondent lovers, plaintive apologies, perplexed fiancés, and melancholy loners.

On the surface Austen's singular novels seem to be delightful romantic fantasies, charming love stories about unlikely couples, but they also contain Austen's profound and sometimes somber satires on society and its manifest hypocrisies. Austen's characters are all politeness, especially when they despise one another, and her stories often writhe with irony as stereotypical social characters display their foolish egocentrisms. Reading Austen's novels makes one keenly of aware of the social traditions that existed during her time.

It would be possible to compare Austen's novels to famous romantic comedies, and it would also be possible to compare them to famous satires, such as Jonathan Swift's brutal *Gulliver's Travels*. Of the two choices, the latter might be more appropriate, as Austen's novels are a kind of incisive literary x-ray device, exposing society's ludicrous habits to a cold derision.

Q: What interest you most about Jane Austen's life?

Pride and Despondence
Michael Clay Thompson

He **conjured** up his courage.   v.
He **fain** would know what surge,   adv.
what **billowed** love, what **fervent**   adj., adj.
thoughts she might return.

Conjectures, nothing more.   n.
She'd never said a word,
no clue, and now he wore
that so-**abashed**, absurd,   adj.

and **plaintive countenance**.   adj., n.
Perplexed, he stood. A fool,   adj.
imagining **entreating** her, **aloof**   n., adj.
and **writhing** in uncertainty, a dance   adj.

of now-**despondent** hopelessness.   adj.
Again he **conjured** up his courage.   v.
He'd speak to her, confess his
hope of marriage, say the words.

Her **amiable** laugh, her air **serene**,   adj., adj.
could cast him down, **dejected**,   adj.
one **prodigious** crash, a scene   adj.
of **melancholy** wreckage.   adj.

He **conjured** up his courage,   v.
resolute; he'd rise above   adj.
this **languor**, cease this dirge,   n.
and state his love.

Classic Words Challenge

In each case below, one of the choices was the word used by the author. Your challenge is to guess which word the author used. This is not a test; it is a game because more than one word choice may work perfectly well. Use your sensitivity and intuition to guess which word the author used. You may need a dictionary.

1. From Jane Austen's *Pride and Prejudice*

   Lydia was Lydia still; untamed, ___________, wild, noisy, and fearless.
   a. plaintive
   b. melancholy
   c. unabashed
   d. amiable

2. From Jane Austen's *Pride and Prejudice*

   The rest of the evening was spent in ________ how soon he would return Mr. Bennet's visit.
   a. conjecturing
   b. reproving
   c. entreating
   d. perplexing

3. From Jane Austen's *Emma*

   You could not give me a greater ___________ for the mistake I fell into.
   a. fervor
   b. billow
   c. conjecture
   d. reproof

4. From Jane Austen's *Emma*

   I do really think Mr. Martin a very ___________ young man.
   a. plaintive
   b. amiable
   c. serene
   d. perplexed

Classic Grammar • Parts of Speech

Every vocabulary word is a part of speech, and every sentence is made of vocabulary. To use vocabulary correctly, we must use it grammatically. Many words can be used in several ways.

In the sentences below, you will find our classic vocabulary words, but they may be present as a different part of speech. In other words, you may see a classic adjective we know but in its adverb form or noun form. Think flexibly. On the lines below sentences three through seven, write the part of speech of each word.

1. He could hear the tattered man bleating **plaintively**. (Crane)

   pron.   v.   v.   adj.   adj.   n.   adj.   adv.

   ____

2. I would **fain** say something. (Thoreau)

   pron.   v.   adv.   v.   pron.

   ____

3. The Martian...walked **serenely** over their guns. (Wells)

   adj.   n.   v.   adv.   prep.   adj.   n.

   ____

4. It was his **amiable** nature. (Dickens)

   pron.   v.   adj.   adj.   n.

   ____

5. Their shape was very **singular** and deformed. (Swift)

   adj.   n.   v.   adv.   adj.   conj.   adj.

   ____

6. The **conjecture** of Major Hewward was true. (Cooper)

   adj.   n.   prep.   -------------n.------------   v.   adj.

   ____

7. **Abashed** glances of servile wonder were exchanged.... (Melville)

   adj.   n.   prep.   adj.   n.   v.   v.

   ____

Classic Word Muddles

In most of the sentences below, one of the classic words is misused, which means that it is a part of speech error. Can you explain the vocabulary/grammar errors? Some of the sentences contain no errors.

1. Dickens was uncertain, but he made a **conjecture**.   correct
2. The odd character **melancholied** the weary traveler.   not a word
3. The **fervor** attitude showed Austen's deep concern.   not an adj.
4. Thoreau looked again at the **perplexed** visitor.   correct
5. Everyone thought that Crane was an **amiable**.   not a n.
6. The typical object was very common and **singular**.   It can't be both.
7. A wonderful **serene** filled Brontë's description.   not a n.
8. Miss Bennet **entreated** Darcy to explain his remark.   correct
9. David Copperfield resented the undeserved **reprove**.   not a n.
10. The cagy old **conjure** winked at the group.   not a n.

Classic Centuries: *abashed*

Below are examples of how *abashed* has been used through the centuries. Which is your favorite?

1952 Ralph Ellison, *Invisible Man*
      "Then I saw the foolish, abashed expression on Wrestrum's face...."
1906 Upton Sinclair, *The Jungle*
      "It would abash the most cynical, it would terrify the most selfish."
1878 Thomas Hardy, *The Return of the Native*
      "...at moments between her exultations she was abashed and blushful."
1850 Charles Dickens, *David Copperfield*
      "He appeared abashed by my aunt's indignant tears."
1847 Emily Brontë, *Wuthering Heights*
      "Hindley descended more leisurely, sobered and abashed."
1792 Mary Wollstonecraft, *Vindication of the Rights of Woman*
      "...a poor timid creature, abashed by a sense of her former weakness."
1667 John Milton, *Paradise Lost*
      "They heard, and were abasht, and up they sprung."

An Impression, Influenced by Jane Austen's *Pride and Prejudice*

In the story below, most of the classic words are used well, but two are not. It may be the meaning that is wrong, or it may be the grammar/usage. Please circle the two classic words that are not used correctly.

As Elizabeth thought about the aristocratic Darcy with his impassive countenance, a myriad of conflicting emotions came to her mind. Had he been more amiable when first they met, she might have found him singularly handsome, but she quickly formed a poor opinion of him as she observed his proud and aloof aura of self-importance. At the community dance, in spite of her friends' profuse entreaties for him to dance, he had seemed to writhe in distaste, refusing all requests and saying that he was not fain to engage in minor entertainments. Her **conjecture** ideas of his real feelings were unpleasant to contemplate.

Minor...the very word irritated her, and a billow of indignation rose in her heart. She herself lacked a fervor for dancing, but she always joined in benevolently, lest her friends think she was supercilious or arrogant. But now the entire affair left her dejected, perplexed. She even felt somewhat abashed, though she knew it was not her fault that this elegant stranger had offended her friends. She was not afraid to reprove him, that was certain, even if he were a prodigious phenomenon of arrogance. She felt profound melancholy as she thought of him.

For some time her feelings adhered resolutely to this problem of Darcy, and she felt in some ways despondent, knowing that it was hopeless to change such a man with such a fortune. In her intuition, something felt like an alarm, and every thought of confronting this tall stranger seemed a portent of danger. But her irritation with his rude behavior did not dissipate, and she was resolute to rebuke him for his manifest indifference to her society.

At any rate, she did not desire his good opinion, and she certainly had never sought it consciously. Even an insult from the proud Darcy would bring no audible **plaintive** from her. As she contemplated the conversation that was looming, she began to conjure her spirit of bravery and self-assurance. That tall Darcy, she promised herself, would find no languid weakling in her; he would learn how it feels to be addressed by an equal.

Classic Words Character

Let us use some of the words that we are learning. Pretend that you are writing a novel, and write a short description of a character, using some of the words in this lesson. Here is an example:

Marco was an amiable soul. Billows of benevolent dreams rose in his imagination, and he conjured up myriad plans for the things he would accomplish and the good he would do in his life. His attitude perplexed his friends, who thought primarily of the money they would make.

Classic Words Place

Now write a short description of a place, a landscape, or a scene, using some of the words in this lesson. Here is an example:

The plaintive cry of a seabird sounded over the tide, and crabs scurried with fervor across the wet sand. The sky had a melancholy cast to it, not bright and happy but somber and gray. The wind made an audible hiss as it blew inland over the tops of the waves, and the ocean seemed to lay prostrate over the earth, looking down into the depths.

Classic Words Invention

Finally, write a short description of something or someone that you imagine, using some of the words in this lesson. Here is an example:

Loneliness is a relative thing. Being alone can be a melancholy experience, or it can be an opportunity to experience the myriad phenomena that the natural world has to offer. Being alone can be serene, providing time for personal conjecture about the meaning of life and about one's singular place in the universe. Of course, the state of loneliness can also stir up a profuse load of memories, some of which might be better forgotten.

JANE AUSTEN'S WRITING TABLE

STEPHEN CRANE

Classic Words – Lesson III

Ten New Words

morose: sullen

droll: amusing

confound: to perplex

wince: to shrink involuntarily

diffidence: lack of confidence

jovial: cheerful

listless: uninterested

sallow: sickly yellow

grimace: a sharp expression

evince: to show

Ten Review Words

Caesar's English I

exquisite: beautifully made

acute: sharp

condescend: to patronize

grotesque: distorted

allude: indirectly refer to

Caesar's English II

ostentatious: showy

inexorable: inevitable

indolent: lazy

doleful: mournful

alacrity: eagerness

morose: adj., mor-OSE, rhymes with *gross*

The adjective **morose** means sullen, in a gloomy or foul mood. In *The Call of the Wild*, Jack London wrote that "He became more morose and irritable." In Stephen Crane's *The Red Badge of Courage*, we read that "The third captive sat with a morose countenance."

droll: adj., DROLE, rhymes with *hole*

The adjective **droll** means oddly amusing. The noun form is *drollery*. In William Makepeace Thackeray's *Vanity Fair*, we read, "She laughed, and the Major did too, at his droll figure on donkey-back, with his long legs touching the ground." In *Heart of Darkness*, Joseph Conrad wrote that "There was a touch of insanity in the proceeding, a sense of lugubrious drollery in the sight."

confound: v., con-FOUND, rhymes with *around*

The verb **confound** means to confuse, to surprise by doing something unexpected, or it means to mix something up. In *Emma*, Jane Austen wrote that "You must not confound us with London in general, my dear sir." Benjamin Franklin wrote in his *Autobiography* that "He was to preach the doctrines, and I was to confound all opponents." In James Baldwin's *Go Tell It on the Mountain*, we read that "they were a little ashamed and confounded before his purity."

wince: n. or v., rhymes with *since*

A **wince** is a small, quick, involuntary grimace of pain or distress. It can also be used as a verb. In Oscar Wilde's *The Picture of Dorian Gray*, we read that "He winced at the mention of his grandfather." In *Dracula*, Bram Stoker wrote that "As we passed along, the gravel hurt my feet, and Lucy noticed me wince." In *I Know Why the Caged Bird Sings*, Maya Angelou wrote, "I winced to picture them sewing the coarse material under a coal-oil lamp with fingers stiffening from the day's work."

diffidence: n., DIFF-ih-dence, rhymes with *evidence*

The noun **diffidence** means lack of confidence. The adjective form is *diffident*. In Jane Austen's *Pride and Prejudice*, we read that "This naturally introduced a panegyric from Jane on his diffidence, and the little value he put on his own good qualities." In *A Tale of Two Cities*, Charles Dickens wrote that "He spoke with the diffidence of a man who knew how slight a thing would overset the delicate organization of the mind."

jovial: adj., JOE-vee-al, rhymes with *alluvial*

The adjective **jovial** means cheerful, as being under the good influence of the planet Jupiter (Jove). In *Macbeth*, William Shakespeare wrote, "Sleek o'er your rugged looks; be bright and jovial among your guests tonight." In Charles Dickens's *David Copperfield*, we read that "I never saw anybody so jovial as Mr. Micawber was." In *Vanity Fair*, William Makepeace Thackeray wrote that "She was the most hospitable and jovial of old vestals."

listless: adj., LIST-less, rhymes with *worthless*

The adjective **listless** means lacking energy, apathetic. In *The Wind in the Willows*, Kenneth Grahame described a character who is "wide awake indeed, but listless, silent, and dejected." Emily Brontë wrote in *Wuthering Heights*, "In vapid listlessness I leant my head against the window."

sallow: adj., SALL-ow, rhymes with *shallow*

The adjective **sallow** refers to an unhealthy yellow or brownish color, usually of the face. In George Eliot's *Silas Marner*, we read, "Here and there a sallow, begrimed face looked out from a gloomy doorway at the strangers." In *The Sun Also Rises*, Ernest Hemingway wrote that "His face had the sallow, yellow look it got when he was insulted."

grimace: n. or v., GRIM-uss, rhymes with *premise*

The noun or verb **grimace** refers to an ugly, twisted facial expression, usually of disgust or pain. In *The Time Machine*, H.G. Wells's Time Traveller says, "I made threatening grimaces at her, and she simply laughed at them." In *Roll of Thunder, Hear My Cry*, Mildred Taylor wrote that "He stood up, his face grimacing with pain." George Eliot, in *Silas Marner*, wrote, "Here the vivacious doctor made a pathetic grimace."

evince: v., ee-VINCE, rhymes with *convince*

The verb **evince** means to show, to reveal. In Mark Twain's *The Prince and the Pauper*, we read that "Tom began to evince a growing distress." In *The Call of the Wild*, Jack London wrote that "Thornton stood between him and Buck, and evinced no intention of getting out of the way."

Stephen Crane

The ability to read academic nonfiction is one of the most important elements of academic success. For practice, here is a short nonfiction essay that contains many of the classic words of this lesson.

When Stephen Crane died in 1900 at the age of only twenty-eight, he was admired by the greatest writers of his time, including Joseph Conrad and H.G. Wells, who called Crane the "best writer of our generation." Crane's masterpiece—now a classic of American fiction—was *The Red Badge of Courage*, a singular novel about the profound transformation of a young man, Henry Fleming, who joins the Union Army during the Civil War.

The Red Badge of Courage follows Henry's emotional and psychological growth as he matures from a jovial recruit, fervent about the glory of war, to an experienced combat veteran who wants not war but serene peace. Stephen Crane's exquisite descriptions of battle were not based on personal experience. He had never been to war, but his imagination was so acute that war veterans praised his descriptions of the doleful phenomena of war, with its myriad horrors and confounding terrors. With droll irony, Crane described condescending officers, troops indolent and listless in the summer heat, morose feelings of despondence, the billowing, prodigious concussions of cannons, wounded men writhing on the battlefield, plaintive cries for help, the feeling of inexorable doom, and agonies that make readers wince and grimace.

The turning point occurs when Henry Fleming panics in battle and flees to the shelter of the forest. There he encounters a sallow, grotesque corpse, which, even though it is horrific, is not as bad as his terrified imagination. He acquires a truer sense of death, his melancholy dissipates, and abashed by his panic, he rebukes himself, turning back toward the battle. No longer the diffident youth pretending to be brave, Henry fights resolutely and achieves the respect of his fellow soldiers. By that time, however, Henry no longer wants to be a hero; he wants green meadows, cool brooks, and eternal peace.

This mature wisdom gives *The Red Badge of Courage* its lasting meaning. Henry has grown from the hero-fantasies of boys to the peaceful dreams of a strong man. Crane himself, dying at such a young age, may never have attained the wisdom his character evinces.

Q: What is the most interesting idea in this essay?

The Red Shame of Desertion

Michael Clay Thompson

Fire flashed from the enemy front,
billows of musket blasts, shattering   n.
the listless moroseness into confounding   adj., n., adj.
fear, the crazed faces of the men sallow   adj.
as bullets whizzed and whacked,
and the youth grimaced in fear, as though struck,   v.
evincing imaginary wounds, contorting   adj.
into grotesque and awkward diffidence   adj., n.
as the roar of the inexorable enemy rose   adj.
from the sunken fence over there,
and the youth dropped his droll   adj.
and foolish jokes, the fear freezing
his limbs, his callow condescension and pride   n.
now shattered and replaced by tremulous
writhings and glances to the rear.   n.
Surely a smart guy would bolt for cover;
to stay was madness; it was obvious; he broke,
turned, stumbled as bullets grazed
his shoulders, and his gaping countenance   n.
sought for assurance from anyone, but the blast
of battle bellowed about, like a portent of doom,   n.
and then he ran, and scurried, and ran, leaping
for the safety of leaves, leaving those stupid
men to die at the fence, those fools who
had not his acute wisdom to run now,   adj.
and into the black of the forest he ran,
wincing with terror as he cracked into branches,   adj.
his fervor for war all past, and prodigious doom   n., adj.
grabbed at his back, a sharp-toothed phenomenon,   n.
and he ran. He would pause, later,
to reprove himself, to know the doleful despondence adv., adj. n.
of the red shame of desertion.

Classic Words Challenge

In each case below, one of the choices was the word used by the author. Your challenge is to guess which word the author used. This is not a test; it is a game because more than one word choice may work perfectly well. Use your sensitivity and intuition to guess which word the author used. You may need a dictionary.

1. From Stephen Crane's *The Red Badge of Courage*

    The third captive sat with a ______________ countenance.
       a. grotesque
       b. morose
       c. listless
       d. droll

2. From Jane Austen's *Emma*

    She was always quick and assured; Isabella slow and ______________.
       a. morose
       b. abashed
       c. jovial
       d. diffident

3. From Stephen Crane's *The Red Badge of Courage*

    He threw a pine cone at a ______________ squirrel.
       a. droll
       b. listless
       c. jovial
       d. sallow

4. From Stephen Crane's *The Red Badge of Courage*

    Other men, punched by bullets, fell in ______________ agonies.
       a. grotesque
       b. diffident
       c. morose
       d. sallow

Classic Grammar • Parts of Speech

Every vocabulary word is a part of speech, and every sentence is made of vocabulary. To use vocabulary correctly, we must use it grammatically. Many words can be used in several ways.

In the sentences below, you will find our classic vocabulary words, but they may be present as a different part of speech. In other words, you may see a classic adjective we know but in its adverb form or noun form. Think flexibly. On the lines below sentences three through seven, write the part of speech of each word.

1. He   was   a   gloomy,   **morose**   fellow. (London)
    pron.   v.   adj.   adj.   adj.   n.

2. Mrs. Linton   eyed   him   with   a   **droll**   expression. (E. Brontë)
    ----------n.----------   v.   pron.   prep.   adj.   adj.   n.

3. He   **winced**   at   the   mention   of   his   grandfather. (Wilde)
    pron.   v.   prep.   adj.   n.   prep.   adj.   n.

4. Here   the   vivacious   doctor   made   a   pathetic   **grimace**. (Eliot)
    adv.   adj.   adj.   n.   v.   adj.   adj.   n.

5. He   was   nonplused,   **evincing**   a   confusion. (Melville)
    pron.   v.   adj.   adj.   adj.   n.

6. This   remark   sobered   the   father's   **joviality**. (Twain)
    adj.   n.   v.   adj.   n.   n.

7. A   tall,   dark-eyed,   **sallow**   woman   half   rose   from   a   couch. (Stowe)
    adj.   adj.   adj.   adj.   n.   adv.   v.   prep.   adj.   n.

Classic Word Muddles

In most of the sentences below, one of the classic words is misused, which means that it is a part of speech error. Can you explain the vocabulary/grammar errors? Some of the sentences contain no errors.

1. Henry made a **grimace** countenance.   not an adj.
2. The general mood among the troops was **morosely**.   not an adv.
3. His **jovial** good humor made him popular in the brigade.   correct
4. Henry's doleful spirit grew full of **diffident**.   not a n.
5. Henry laughed **droll** at the sergeant's error.   not an adv.
6. The situation **grotesqued** into madness.   not a word
7. His actions **evinced** no feelings of despondence.   correct
8. The inexperienced corporal was a true **condescending**.   not a n.
9. His face was sickly and **sallow**.   correct
10. The clever remark was actually a sly **allude**.   not a n.

Classic Centuries: *sallow*

Below are examples of how *sallow* has been used through the centuries. Which is your favorite?

1911   Edith Wharton, *Ethan Frome*
        "Her narrow lips were of the same sallow colour as her face."

1900   Joseph Conrad, *Lord Jim*
        "His clean-shaved cheeks were large and sallow."

1895   Thomas Hardy, *Jude the Obscure*
        "She beheld a foreigner with black hair and a sallow face."

1861   George Eliot, *Silas Marner*
        "Here and there a sallow, begrimed face looked out from a gloomy
        doorway at the strangers."

1854   Charles Dickens, *Hard Times*
        "His face, close-shaven, thin, and sallow, was shaded by a great
        quantity of dark hair."

1847   Charlotte Brontë, *Jane Eyre*
        "His complexion was singularly sallow."

1596   William Shakespeare, *Romeo and Juliet*
        "What a deal of brine / Hath washed thy sallow cheeks for Rosaline."

An Impression, Influenced by Stephen Crane's *The Red Badge of Courage*

In the story below, most of the classic words are used well, but two are not. It may be the meaning that is wrong, or it may be the grammar/usage. Please circle the two classic words that are not used correctly.

His mother had entreated him not to enlist. But Henry's mind had soared with images of his future heroism. He envisioned himself as a jovial Union soldier in a handsome blue uniform, confident, leading the charge with alacrity and receiving the admiration of all the sallow-faced troops in his unit. "That Henry," they would say as the cannon smoke began to dissipate, "he is something." "Boys," he would answer in amiable condescension, "I'm just doing my duty." The **languor** soldiers would grow silent in admiration before sinking back into their listless and diffident tedium. It was an exquisite vision, this heroic moment of his.

But now his mother was overwhelmed with grief and fear. She was despondent, sobbing morosely about his never coming back. Her suffering was so acute that even Henry was confounded, not knowing how to evince his invulnerability. Of course he would come back. He winced as her tears fell down her cheeks, and he avoided a droll joke about her needless fear.

"Don't worry, Ma," he said, but she grimaced as she raised her eyes to the heavens. The grotesque image of his terrified mother disturbed him. Why could she not understand: He was Henry, soon to be Henry the hero. There was no reason to be melancholy. He would return from war triumphantly, to the fervent admiration of the town. Billows of praise would come from the assembled crowds, and he would be fain to appreciate their esteem.

His dejected mother wanted none of that. "Don't try to fight the whole battle by yourself, Henry," she reproved him plaintively. "You're just one little fella amongst a whole lot of others."

One little fella. Those words burned his pride, and he writhed inwardly, abashed at such a rebuke. In his inexperience, he conjured up images of fierce firefights, with himself as the resolute leader charging ostentatiously through a hailstorm of bullets. The perplexed enemy would hesitate, gasp, and begin a terrified retreat. It would be a **singular**. His countenance beamed with pride to think of the courage he would manifest.

Real battle would prove different than his boyish imagination expected.

Classic Words Character

Let us use some of the words that we are learning. Pretend that you are writing a novel, and write a short description of a character, using some of the words in this lesson. Here is an example:

The stranger strode into the room from the cold, dark outside, a condescending sneer on his face, a kind of wince, a sallow displeasure at seeing us standing in a group. There was something grotesque in his ostentatious glare, as though we were nothing but an indolent and listless pack of useless beings. We said nothing, and he turned and left.

Classic Words Place

Now write a short description of a place, a landscape, or a scene, using some of the words in this lesson. Here is an example:

The burning dunes stretched to the horizon in every direction from the wrecked aircraft, evincing the hopelessness of either escape or rescue. No shade, no shadow, no water broke the exquisite perfection of the desert, with its inexorable powers of dehydration and exhaustion. The sun began to go down with a final, shocking blaze, and somewhere in the distance, a desert creature cried its doleful cry.

Classic Words Invention

Finally, write a short description of something or someone that you imagine, using some of the words in this lesson. Here is an example:

To be concise is to avoid the perils of ostentatious wordiness, the grotesque excess of superfluous syllables, the horrid piles of adjectives and adverbs that make one grimace in distaste. Better is the jovial perfection of the right noun predicated by its right verb in exquisite precision.

STEEL PEN, LATE NINETEENTH CENTURY

MARY SHELLEY

Classic Words – Lesson IV

Ten New Words

expostulate: to object earnestly

deprecate: to deplore

demure: modest and shy

wan: pallid or weak

reproach: accuse, blame, rebuke

din: a racket

eddy: a swirl or whirlpool

injunction: a command or prohibition

expedient: a convenient means

decorum: proper behavior

Ten Review Words

Caesar's English I

placid: calm

vex: to irritate

clamor: outcry

venerate: to respect

incredulous: skeptical

Caesar's English II

oblique: indirect or slanting

pensive: thoughtful

magnanimous: generous

importune: to pester

peremptory: dictatorial

expostulate: v., ex-POSS-tyoo-late, second syllable rhymes with *boss*

The verb **expostulate** means to express strong disagreement, to object earnestly. The noun form is *expostulation*. In *Jude the Obscure*, Thomas Hardy wrote that "His arm was held back by an expostulating woman." In *Frankenstein*, Mary Shelley described how a character "attempted to expostulate with her father, but he left her angrily, reiterating his tyrannical mandate."

deprecate: v., DEPP-reh-kate, rhymes with *celebrate*

The verb **deprecate** means to disparage, to deplore. The noun form is *deprecation*. In Mary Shelley's *Frankenstein*, we read, "I learned, from the views of social life which it developed, to admire their virtues, and to deprecate the vices of mankind." In his great poem *Leaves of Grass*, Walt Whitman wrote that "We have had ducking and deprecating about enough."

demure: adj., deh-MYOOR, rhymes with *literature*

The adjective **demure** refers to a person (usually a woman) who is modest and shy. In *Vanity Fair*, William Makepeace Thackeray wrote that "When attacked sometimes, Becky had a knack of adopting a demure ingenue air, under which she was most dangerous." In *Ivanhoe*, Sir Walter Scott referred to the "black dresses, bare scalps, and demure looks of these churchmen."

wan: adj., WAHN, rhymes with *lawn*

The adjective **wan** refers to a pallid or sickly pale tone. It often but not always refers to the face, and it can imply weakness as in illness. In Emily Brontë's *Wuthering Heights*, we read that "Her countenance grew wan with watching and sorrow." In Toni Morrison's *Song of Solomon*, "She tried desperately to normalize the situation, smiling wanly and blinking her eyes, searching for words and manners and civilization."

reproach: v. or n., ree-PROACH, rhymes with *approach*

To **reproach** is to accuse, to express disapproval. The word can also be used as a noun. In Thomas Hardy's *The Return of the Native*, a character says, "If I had known you wished to call me up here only to reproach me, I wouldn't have come." In Stephen Crane's *The Red Badge of Courage*, we read that "The spectral soldier was at his side like a stalking reproach."

din: n., rhymes with *tin*

The noun **din** means a racket: a loud, unpleasant, lasting noise. In *Paradise Lost*, John Milton described "the odious din of War." In *The Jungle*, Sinclair Lewis wrote, "and then off they went amid a din of cheers." H.G. Wells, in *The War of the Worlds*, described the "deafening and confusing conflict of noises—the clangorous din of the Martians."

eddy: n. or v., EDD-ee, rhymes with *ready*

An **eddy** is a swirl or whirlpool; the word can also be a verb. In *The Red Badge of Courage*, Stephen Crane wrote that "As the smoke eddied away, the youth saw that the charge had been repulsed." In *The Call of the Wild*, Jack London described how "they swung the raft into the big eddy by the sawmill at Dawson." In *Lord Jim*, Joseph Conrad wrote, "I thought of a dry leaf imprisoned in an eddy of wind."

injunction: n., in-JUNK-shun, rhymes with *compunction*

The noun **injunction** refers to a formal, authoritative order, often one that prohibits something, as an injunction against something. In Charles Dickens's *David Copperfield*, we read about a letter that "was addressed to myself and laid an injunction on me, in a few affectionate words, never to refer to the subject of that evening." Mary Shelley, in *Frankenstein*, wrote that "my father's dying injunction had forbidden my uncle to allow me to embark in a seafaring life."

expedient: n., ex-PEE-dee-ent, rhymes with *ingredient*

The noun **expedient** refers to a convenient—possibly immoral—means to an end. Another noun form is *expediency*. In Marjorie Rawlings's *The Yearling*, we read that "It had never occurred to him that one man could get the best of another by the simple expedient of telling him the truth." Frederick Douglass, in his *Narrative*, wrote that "He was asked by Colonel Lloyd and my old master, why he resorted to this extraordinary expedient."

decorum: n., deh-KORR-um, rhymes with *forum*

The noun **decorum** refers to proper behavior, conducted with taste and propriety. The adjective form is *decorous*. In Herman Melville's *Billy Budd*, we read that "Billy's action was a terrible breach of naval decorum." E.M. Forster, in *A Passage to India*, wrote that "the Guest House party were departing next morning, as decorum required."

Mary Shelley

The ability to read academic nonfiction is one of the most important elements of academic success. For practice, here is a short nonfiction essay that contains many of the classic words of this lesson.

Nothing about the venerated English novelist Mary Shelley was ordinary. Her talent, background, education, and marriage were all extraordinary, and each element contributed to her literary masterpiece, *Frankenstein: or, The Modern Prometheus.*

The daughter of famous intellectuals Mary Wollstonecraft and William Godwin, Mary Godwin received an exceptional education from her father, a pensive and brilliant political philosopher. She never knew her mother, who died just eleven days after she was born.

At the age of nineteen, Mary married Percy Shelley, the great British poet. Traveling in Switzerland with their friend George Gordon, Lord Byron, Mary conjured from the eddies of her imagination a story of melancholy horror: a grotesque creature with a horrid countenance made of pieces of bodies, re-animated to life by electricity. The profound idea so impressed Shelley and Byron that they importuned Mary with peremptory alacrity to develop the story into a full-length novel.

The result was that Mary wrote a singular literary phenomenon, a melancholy novel of a grotesque monster, isolated in a prodigious loneliness and despondence, deprecated by incredulous villagers who clamor for his death. The sallow creature is abhorred even by his own creator, Dr. Frankenstein, and is hounded and rejected by all of humanity. At one point in the novel, the dejected creature expostulates with Frankenstein to be magnanimous and to build him a friend, then retreats in incredulous fury when Frankenstein refuses his entreaties.

The endurance of Mary Shelley's *Frankenstein* rests on a paradox—that it is the morose monster with his horrid countenance who is the person, and the cruel people who are the monsters. The monster flees from the crushing din of social rejection, and the people, for all of their decorum, are exposed as grimacing brutes. The novel thus raises profound questions about the essence of human nature.

Q: What does this essay make you wonder?

The Monster in the Snow

Michael Clay Thompson

The creature creeped about the hut,
his **sallow countenance** a mask   adj., n.
of longing **clamoring** inside.   adj.
No person, he, but what
he was, a beast, a rascal,
well, he sometimes **writhed**   v.
in pensive agony, when looking in a glass
he saw his monster-face.

Incredulous, it made him feel,   adj.
and full of self-**reproach**,   n.
and **eddies** of **perplexity** would whirl   n., n.
around his heart, his gauche
and pre-owned heart. He'd steal
a different heart, if ere he could;
he'd poach one from some **placid** fool—   adj.
well, no, he wouldn't really, couldn't
violate **decorum** so. Some inner rule,   n.
the sharp **injunction**, told him no.   n.

So now, he'd hulk outside the hut,
and listless, lean against the driving snow,
and lug the firewood to their door, so shut
against him, his heart expostulating so:
be **resolute**, just knock and knock   adj.
against the door that now was locked
against him, the **pensive** monster in the snow,   adj.
with **diffident** and **grotesque**   adj., adj.
monster-face.

Classic Words Challenge

In each case below, one of the choices was the word used by the author. Your challenge is to guess which word the author used. This is not a test; it is a game because more than one word choice may work perfectly well. Use your sensitivity and intuition to guess which word the author used. You may need a dictionary.

1. From Mary Shelley's *Frankenstein*

    She attempted to ___________ with her father....
    a. deprecate
    b. reproach
    c. clamor
    d. expostulate

2. From Mary Shelley's *Frankenstein*

    Our ________ home and our contented hearts are regulated by the same immutable laws.
    a. placid
    b. incredulous
    c. wan
    d. demure

3. From Mary Shelley's *Frankenstein*

    I learned...to admire their virtues, and to _______ the vices of mankind.
    a. expostulate
    b. venerate
    c. deprecate
    d. reproach

4. From Harriet Beecher Stowe's *Uncle Tom's Cabin*

    I became a piece of drift-wood, and have been... ____ about, ever since.
    a. eddying
    b. deprecating
    c. expostulating
    d. reproaching

Classic Grammar • Parts of Speech

Every vocabulary word is a part of speech, and every sentence is made of vocabulary. To use vocabulary correctly, we must use it grammatically. Many words can be used in several ways.

In the sentences below, you will find our classic vocabulary words, but they may be present as a different part of speech. In other words, you may see a classic adjective we know but in its adverb form or noun form. Think flexibly. On the lines below sentences three through seven, write the part of speech of each word.

1.   I **expostulated** with him but in vain. (Swift)

    pron.   v.   prep.   pron.   conj.   prep.   n.

2.   But the other made a **deprecating** gesture. (Crane)

    conj.   adj.   n.   v.   adj.   adj.   n.

3.   She cast her eyes down **demurely**.... (Thackeray)

    pron.   v.   adj.   n.   adv.   adv.

4.   The **expedient** was not without its use. (Cooper)

    adj.   n.   v.   adv.   prep.   adj.   n.

5.   His warning voice was unheard, for the **din**. (Scott)

    adj.   adj.   n.   v.   adj.   prep.   adj.   n.

6.   Elizabeth would not oppose such an **injunction**. (Austen)

    n.   v.   adv.   v.   adj.   adj.   n.

7.   Even her triumph was measured and **decorous**. (James)

    adv.   adj.   n.   v.   adj.   conj.   adj.

Classic Word Muddles

In most of the sentences below, one of the classic words is misused, which means that it is a part of speech error. Can you explain the vocabulary/grammar errors? Some of the sentences contain no errors.

1. A simple **expedient** solved Frankenstein's problem. — correct
2. She urgently expressed her **expostulate** objection. — not an adj.
3. The **eddy** current swept away all of the evidence. — not an adj.
4. The monster recoiled at the **vex** situation. — not an adj.
5. The innocent person was a true **demure**. — not a n.
6. The villagers **venerated** the famous scientist. — correct
7. A loud **clamor** came from the disappointed crowd. — correct
8. The day slowly dissolved into a deep blue **placid**. — not a n.
9. She angrily **reproached** him for his forgetfulness. — correct
10. They never repeated the **deprecate** mistake. — not an adj.

Classic Centuries: *wan*

Below are examples of how *wan* has been used through the centuries. Which is your favorite?

1925   F. Scott Fitzgerald, *The Great Gatsby*
"Her wan, scornful mouth smiled."

1895   H.G. Wells, *The Time Machine*
"The sea stretched away to the south-west, to rise into a sharp bright horizon against the wan sky."

1847   Emily Brontë, *Wuthering Heights*
"Her countenance grew wan with watching and sorrow."

1826   James Fenimore Cooper, *The Last of the Mohicans*
"A gleam of light from the opening crossed his wan countenance."

1816   Mary Shelley, *Frankenstein*
"I sat watching the wan countenance of my friend—his eyes half closed, and his limbs hanging listlessly."

1601   William Shakespeare, *Hamlet*
"That from her working all his visage wanned, tears in his eyes...."

1385   Geoffrey Chaucer, *The Canterbury Tales*
"Myn is the drenching in the see so wan."

An Impression, Influenced by Mary Shelley's *Frankenstein*

In the story below, most of the classic words are used well, but three are not. It may be the meaning that is wrong, or it may be the grammar/usage. Please circle the three classic words that are not used correctly.

You may conjecture how I reproached myself for every breach of decorum that I committed. Because of the hideous way I had been created, I knew nothing of social manners or the **injunction** rules, and I crept through the forest, scrounging food and huddling miserably against the cold, feeling prodigious billows of dejection and despondence. The melancholy din of a howling storm was no stranger to me, and I often deprecated the soul of my aloof creator, the scientist whose very existence was now abhorrent to me.

My soul had no placid or serene center. I was rather a wild thing, vexed by loneliness and inwardly clamoring for the smallest touch of human kindness. I hid in the shadows and observed people living their lives, and in my peremptory heart I secretly venerated every soul whose behavior evinced kindness. My desperate need for a caring, magnanimous word became more profound with each passing day, and I grimaced with incredulity as I realized the extent of my morose isolation.

Nothing I did seemed to relieve my suffering. I could find no expedient to soothe my condition. I hid, I starved, and I leaned against the eddies of snow that blinded my vision. For some time I became absorbed by a single family, envying their love of one another and conjuring, in my pensive imagination, scenes that included me, in which I was accepted and almost adopted, and my happiness became manifest and **expostulated**. But then I would awake from my daydream, and the illusion would dissipate, and I would wince with agony at the realization of my continuing misery.

If only I could know the jovial friendship and family love that I witnessed from afar. If only I could importune a stranger and find a friend. If only the din of human rejection could be silenced from my memories. If only I did not writhe in **acute** as I reflected on the scenes of my actual life. My inner being clamored for something better, something personal and individual, something that meant that I too could have a meaningful human life. My soul cried in plaintive tones for relief.

Classic Words Character

Let us use some of the words that we are learning. Pretend that you are writing a novel, and write a short description of a character, using some of the words in this lesson. Here is an example:

John stood in pensive silence, reflecting on the pointless rules of decorum that he was expected to observe. He was from the casual West Coast and had never experienced the peremptory reproaches of social custom that he faced here, the injunctions against what he regarded as amiable pleasantness. He turned his thinking to more placid questions.

Classic Words Place

Now write a short description of a place, a landscape, or a scene, using some of the words in this lesson. Here is an example:

Eddies of mist rose slowly up the slope, rising above the evergreens that looked over the valley far below. An incredulous hawk circled and then cried, vexed over an escaping mouse. The sky was blue, serene and placid, and the forest had its own decorum, each plant and animal following the rules of the mountain. The early light streaked in its oblique angle down from the sun, flooding the slope with the magnanimous gift of warmth.

Classic Words Invention

Finally, write a short description of something or someone that you imagine, using some of the words in this lesson. Here is an example:

The squirrel perched on the branch, barking its little bark to reproach the dog below on the lawn. The incredulous dog saw the squirrel but did not know how to get to him. A fallen trunk leaning against the tree provided an oblique path upward, but not high enough.

QUILL PEN

FREDERICK DOUGLASS

Classic Words – Lesson V

Ten New Words

affect: to influence

anon: shortly

feign: pretend

eloquence: effective language

wont: habit

benefactor: financial contributor

hitherto: until now

complacence: smug self-satisfaction

interpose: put between

martial: warlike

Ten Review Words

Caesar's English I

tremulous: quivering

apprehension: fear

vivid: bright

abate: to lessen

sublime: lofty

Caesar's English II

tacit: unspoken

affable: friendly

sanguine: cheerfully confident

torpid: sluggish

mortify: profoundly humiliate

affect: v., ah-FEKT, rhymes with *respect*

The verb **affect** means to influence, to have an effect, or to pretend. Someone who pretends can be described as affected or to have an affectation. Do not use the noun *impact* as a verb; use *affect*. In Maya Angelou's *I Know Why the Caged Bird Sings*, we read that "he stopped his affected way of talking." In *Treasure Island*, Robert Louis Stevenson wrote that "you can never tell what will affect the superstitious."

anon: adv., ah-NON, rhymes with *baton*

The archaic adverb **anon** means shortly. In *The Hound of the Baskervilles*, Arthur Conan Doyle wrote, "anon their bemused wits awoke to the nature of the deed." In William Shakespeare's *A Midsummer Night's Dream*, we read that "Our Queen and all her elves come here anon."

feign: v., FAYNE, rhymes with *strain*

The verb **feign** means to pretend that you are affected by something. In *Native Son*, Richard Wright wrote, "'What's the matter?' he asked, feigning ignorance." In *The Red Badge of Courage*, Stephen Crane described "an old fellow who used to sit upon a cracker box in front of the store and feign to despise such exhibitions." In Mildred Taylor's *Roll of Thunder, Hear My Cry*, we read that "the three of us forced ourselves to stare into the fire in feigned disinterest."

eloquence: n., ELL-oh-kwence, rhymes with *intelligence*

The noun **eloquence** refers to fluent, persuasive language. The adjective is *eloquent*, and the adverb is *eloquently*. In H.G. Wells's *The War of the Worlds*, we read that "He talked so eloquently of the possibility of capturing a Martian fighting-machine...." In *Rebecca of Sunnybrook Farm*, Kate Douglas Wiggin wrote, "Miranda said nothing as she closed the door, but her looks were at once equivalent to and more eloquent than words."

wont: n., WANT, rhymes with *font*

The noun **wont** refers to one's habit, one's custom, one's typical behavior. We also use the adjective forms *wont* or *wonted* (accustomed). In Nathaniel Hawthorne's *The Scarlet Letter*, we read that a character "could not find her wonted place." In *King Lear*, William Shakespeare wrote, "your Highness is not entertained with that ceremonious affection as you were wont."

benefactor: n., BEN-eh-fack-tor, rhymes with *tractor*

The noun **benefactor** refers to a patron, to someone who contributes money or other assistance. A female benefactor is a benefactress, and the support provided is a benefaction. In *Great Expectations*, Charles Dickens wrote that "I had discovered my real benefactor."

hitherto: adv., HIH-ther-TOO, rhymes with *residue*

The adverb **hitherto** means previously, until now, until a point in time. In *Kidnapped*, Robert Louis Stevenson described "the man of the house, who had hitherto pretended to have no English." In *Walden*, Henry David Thoreau wrote that "I have hitherto indulged very little in philanthropic enterprises." In Jane Austen's *Emma*, we read that "even if I have not underrated him hitherto, he may yet turn out well."

complacent: adj., kom-PLAY-sent, rhymes with *adjacent*

The adjective **complacent** refers to smug self-satisfaction. The noun form is *complacency*, and the adverb form is *complacently*. In Charles Dickens's *Great Expectations*, "They showed the complacent forbearance...." Harriet Beecher Stowe, in *Uncle Tom's Cabin*, wrote that "he took it and looked at it with a sharp, complacent air, like a man who thinks he has done about the right thing." In *Why We Can't Wait*, Martin Luther King, Jr., said that we must not "remain complacent in the midst of injustice."

interpose: v., in-ter-POZE, rhymes with *hose*

The verb **interpose** means to place between, to insert, to interrupt, or to intervene. The noun form is *interposition*. In *Wuthering Heights*, Emily Brontë wrote that "She held her hand interposed between the furnace heat and her eyes." In *The Last of the Mohicans*, James Fenimore Cooper described a situation "as if a supernatural agency had interposed in the behalf of Uncas."

martial: adj., MAR-shull, rhymes with *partial*

The adjective **martial** means warlike. In James Fenimore Cooper's *The Last of the Mohicans*, we read about a character of "gray locks and furrowed lineaments, blending with a martial air and tread." In *Hamlet*, William Shakespeare wrote that "Thus twice before, and jump at this dead hour, / With martial stalk hath he gone by our watch."

Frederick Douglass

The ability to read academic nonfiction is one of the most important elements of academic success. For practice, here is a short nonfiction essay that contains many of the classic words of this lesson.

Among the sublime figures of American history, few are more venerated than Frederick Douglass, whose majestic countenance and fierce eloquence affected the country's democratic conscience at a time of profound crisis. Douglass's martial clamor for the end of slavery and for the equality of African-Americans had resonance because of his own life as a self-educated escaped slave. He had lived what he was talking about, and the resolute force of his words—which continue to mortify us—has not abated, more than a hundred years after his death in 1895. "One and God," he said, "make a majority."

In addition to his singular importance in the history of American civil rights, Douglass is also a figure in the history of education. From his earliest years, he apprehended that education was critically important. During his childhood, it was illegal for slaves to read or write, so Douglass had to learn his literacy through subterfuge and affable trickery. Once he could read, his genius propelled him to the front ranks of American democratic thought.

Neither tremulous nor diffident, Douglass deprecated slavery and documented its myriad horrors in his *Narrative of the Life of Frederick Douglass, an American Slave*—an autobiography that is still too vivid in its unabashed descriptions of cruelty to be read by the young or the faint of heart. Douglass's *Narrative* makes the reader wince and grimace with shock at the grotesque and vicious behaviors of slave owners and with the acute suffering of the despondent slaves whose miserable lives were at the mercy of despicable individuals.

Late in Douglass's life, he was nominated for Vice President of the United States on the Equal Rights Party ticket—the first African-American ever to be nominated for the office.

At a time when apologists for American slavery complacently based their arguments on the supposed inferiority of the slaves, Douglass stood like a colossus as a living reproof and refutation of the evil and the torpid stupidity of slavery. His prodigious genius, his moral reproach, and his eloquent leadership helped to drive a stake into the heart of America's most un-American institution.

Q: What is your favorite sentence in this essay? Why?

I Never Saw My Mother
Michael Clay Thompson

I never saw my mother, to know her as such, more
than four or five times in my life; and each of these
times was very short in duration, and at night.
 - Frederick Douglass, *Narrative*

I never saw my mother, no,
no **vivid** face **abates**   adj., v
in **eddies** of my memory.   n.
Soft shadows **dissipate**.   v.

I never saw my mother, oh,
no **countenance sublime**,   n., adj.
now **billows** softly in my thought —   v.
no fragment from that time.

I never saw my mother. Now
I **venerate** a dream,   v.
but **grotesque** facts have **interposed**;   adj., v.
and heart cannot be **feigned**.   v.

I never saw my mother, so
an **eloquence** of pain —   n.
waves **profound, tremulous** and slow,   adj., adj.
despondent — a refrain.   adj.

I never saw my mother, though
she sought me through the night.
A broken-hearted void, **anon**,   adv.
a might-have-been — denied.

Classic Words Challenge

In each case below, one of the choices was the word used by the author. Your challenge is to guess which word the author used. This is not a test; it is a game because more than one word choice may work perfectly well. Use your sensitivity and intuition to guess which word the author used. You may need a dictionary.

1. From Charles Dickens's *David Copperfield*

   You don't remember your own ____________ expressions.
      a. vivid
      b. tremulous
      c. eloquent
      d. martial

2. From George Eliot's *Silas Marner*

   He looked across the table at her with ___________ gravity.
      a. complacent
      b. martial
      c. vivid
      d. feigned

3. From Frederick Douglass's *Narrative*

   I may be deemed superstitious...in regarding this event as a special ______________ of divine Providence in my favor.
      a. eloquence
      b. apprehension
      c. interposition
      d. abatement

4. From Richard Wright's *Native Son*

   "What's the matter?" he asked, ____________ interest.
      a. abating
      b. interposing
      c. affecting
      d. feigning

Classic Grammar • Parts of Speech

Every vocabulary word is a part of speech, and every sentence is made of vocabulary. To use vocabulary correctly, we must use it grammatically. Many words can be used in several ways.

In the sentences below, you will find our classic vocabulary words, but they may be present as a different part of speech. In other words, you may see a classic adjective we know but in its adverb form or noun form. Think flexibly. On the lines below sentences three through seven, write the part of speech of each word.

1. Her **unwonted** joy shrank back, appalled. (Hawthorne)

   adj.   adj.   n.   v.   adv.   adj.

____

2. But **anon** their bemused wits awoke to the nature of the deed. (Doyle)

  conj. adv. adj.   adj.   n.   v. prep. adj. n. prep. adj. n.

____

3. **Hitherto** I have gone on vague lines. (Wells)

     adv.   pron.   v.   v.   prep.   adj.   n.

____

4. Newman was **feigning** a greater confidence than he felt. (James)

    n.   v.   v.   adj. adj.   n.   conj. pron. v.

____

5. It was the most **affecting** sight I have ever seen. (Orwell)

 pron. v. adj. adv.   adj.   n. pron. v.   adv.   v.

____

6. A rolling gray cloud **interposed** as the regiment doggedly replied. (Crane)

 adj. adj.   adj.   n.   v.   conj. adj.   n.   adv.   v.

____

7. Its shades and glens rang with the sound of **martial** music. (Cooper)

 adj. n.   conj. n.   v. prep. adj. n. prep. adj.   n.

____

Classic Word Muddles

In most of the sentences below, one of the classic words is misused, which means that it is a part of speech error. Can you explain the vocabulary/grammar errors? Some of the sentences contain no errors.

1.	She gradually became a smug **complacent**.	not a n.
2.	Douglass was famous for **eloquence** speeches.	not an adj.
3.	The terrible tragedy **affected** everyone profoundly.	correct
4.	We hoped that it would be an **anon** event.	not an adj.
5.	The tall trees waved **tremulous**.	not an adv.
6.	He **interposed** himself between her and the intruder.	correct
7.	He **wonted** to leave the island immediately.	wanted
8.	It was a **feign** sadness, not a real one.	not an adj.
9.	This was a new example, not a **hitherto**.	not a n.
10.	The criminals were arrested by the **martial**.	marshal

Classic Centuries: *benefactor*

Below are examples of how *benefactor* has been used through the centuries. Which is your favorite?

1963   Sylvia Plath, *The Bell Jar*
      "The first time I saw a finger bowl was at the home of my benefactress."

1861   George Eliot, *Silas Marner*
      "He will presently find himself dreaming of a possible benefactor."

1860   Charles Dickens, *Great Expectations*
      "He is the benefactor so long unknown to me."

1860   Charles Dickens, *Great Expectations*
      "She perceived I had discovered my real benefactor."

1847   Emily Brontë, *Wuthering Heights*
      "He was not insolent to his benefactor."

1816   Mary Shelley, *Frankenstein*
      "You were hereafter to be hailed as the benefactors of your species."

1719   Daniel Defoe, *Robinson Crusoe*
      "The first thing I did was to recompense my original benefactor, my good old captain."

An Impression, Influenced by Frederick Douglass's *Narrative*

In the story below, most of the classic words are used well, but one is not. It may be the meaning that is wrong, or it may be the grammar/usage. Please circle the classic word that is not used correctly.

I have not hitherto described my background publicly, but it is time to do so. My earliest memories of life on the Maryland plantation—no eloquence can describe this pain—are incomplete and sometimes dubious, but I vividly remember trying to understand that I was a slave and that I had no family in the sense that my master had. My master was no benefactor, and I cannot affect a fondness for him that I do not feel. With martial command he sent us to the fields at first light, and we worked into the wan gloaming, with little allowance for rest or food. Sometimes we were tremulous with cold, for we were not provided with adequate warm raimants, and our suffering did not abate until the warmth of spring spread over the fields. If any slave dared to expostulate with the master for warmer garments, he stood aloof and reproved the offending slave in the most grotesque tones. I am still mortified by these painful memories.

None of us could read or write; it was against the law for any slave to become literate and for anyone to teach a slave. Our lives were limited to grueling manual labor, and though we affected a **jovial** at times, we were secretly melancholy and morose, despondent over the impossibility of escaping our servitude. Our master complacently imagined that we were content with our misery, though any closer examination of our dejected countenances would have shown him otherwise.

Somehow I understood, even as a small child, that education would be my salvation. The powerful injunction against slave education was proof in my mind that knowledge was important. If slave owners were universally against my education, it must mean that ignorance would keep me in slavery, and that knowledge would mean freedom. I began to venerate the very idea of knowledge. Accordingly, it was my wont to observe all forms of writing, though feigning indifference. Quietly, I inspected the titles of books and newspapers, and began to study every label and sign at the plantation. Sublime moments of apprehension occurred as I associated letters with sounds, and gained the ability to read—one word at a time. I also adopted the expedient of claiming I could read, only to be corrected in condescending rebukes that unknowingly revealed the actual meaning of the words, thus giving me priceless lessons of literacy.

Classic Words Character

Let us use some of the words that we are learning. Pretend that you are writing a novel, and write a short description of a character, using some of the words in this lesson. Here is an example:

The editor stood silently, feigning agreement with the eloquent nonsense she had just heard from the complacent writer. Mortified by the writer's illogical idea, she waited for the protests in her mind to abate before speaking. She knew that she could appear to give tacit approval to such foolish prattle, but she needed a moment to compose her objection.

Classic Words Place

Now write a short description of a place, a landscape, or a scene, using some of the words in this lesson. Here is an example:

The tremulous breeze eddied up from the grasses in the inlet, and the afternoon light began to abate as the sinking sun cast long shadows toward the east. The rich mud of the inlet had a benevolent effect on the grasses, and the wind passed over them as though making a tacit comment. Somewhere a sandpiper issued a sanguine peep that summed up the effect of the vivid late light.

Classic Words Invention

Finally, write a short description of something or someone that you imagine, using some of the words in this lesson. Here is an example:

The aging benefactor listened carefully to the description of the museum. It was not his wont to donate without knowing the facts, but this eloquent explanation put before him, in vivid terms, the good that he could do, and he began to reply, in the most affable manner, that he would help.

SLAVE HOLDING PEN

HENRY DAVID THOREAU

Classic Words – Lesson VI

Ten New Words

patron: a customer or supporter

intervene: to come between

gesticulate: to gesture

haggard: looking exhausted

fastidious: detailed

discomfit: to make uneasy

sage: profoundly wise

plausible: believable

animated: lively

obtrude: to intrude noticeably

Ten Review Words

Caesar's English I

odious: hateful

visage: the face

vulgar: common

subtle: slight

wistful: yearning

Caesar's English II

obsequious: cringing, submissive

ignominy: disgrace

acquiescence: passive compliance

impassive: without emotion

impending: about to happen

patron: n., PAY-tron, rhymes with *matron*

The noun **patron** refers to someone who supports a person or a cause, financially or otherwise. To patronize someone, however, is to treat him or her with kindness but in a condescending manner. The act of being a patron is called patronage. In Aldous Huxley's *Brave New World*, we read that "their smile was rather patronizing." In *The Picture of Dorian Gray*, Oscar Wilde wrote that a character "assured me that I was a munificent patron of art." In *The House of the Seven Gables*, Nathaniel Hawthorne described characters who "evidently considered themselves not merely her equals, but her patrons and superiors."

intervene: v., inter-VEEN, rhymes with *seen*

To **intervene** is to come between, sometimes in a way that changes the outcome, but sometimes not. In *Frankenstein*, Mary Shelley wrote, "I...was beginning to conjecture that some fortunate chance had intervened to prevent the execution of his menaces." In H.G. Wells's *The Invisible Man*, we read that "In five minutes a dozen turnings intervened between me and the costumier's shop."

gesticulate: v., jess-TICK-yoo-late, rhymes with *matriculate*

The verb **gesticulate** means to gesture dramatically. In *The Invisible Man*, H.G. Wells wrote, "For a space people stood amazed and gesticulating." In *The Hound of the Baskervilles*, Arthur Conan Doyle described a man who "gesticulated and danced with excitement."

haggard: adj., HAG-erd, rhymes with *staggered*

The adjective **haggard** means looking exhausted and ill, especially from worry. In James Fenimore Cooper's *The Last of the Mohicans*, we read that "The countenance of Hawkeye was haggard and careworn, and his air dejected." In *Hard Times*, Charles Dickens wrote that "Stephen came out of the hot mill into the damp wind and cold wet streets, haggard and worn."

fastidious: adj., fas-TID-ee-ous, rhymes with *hideous*

The adjective **fastidious** means that someone is extremely or excessively concerned about details such as cleanliness and courtesy. In Charlotte Brontë's *Jane Eyre*, Jane asks, "Is Mr. Rochester an exacting, fastidious sort of man?" In James Fenimore Cooper's *The Last of the Mohicans*, we read that "At length his accurate and fastidious eye seemed satisfied."

discomfit: v., dis-COME-fit, rhymes with *some fit*

The verb **discomfit** means to make someone feel emotionally uncomfortable or uneasy. The adjective form is *discomfited*, and the noun is *discomfiture*. In *Ethan Frome*, Edith Wharton wrote that "Ethan smiled at the discomfiture he had caused." In William Makepeace Thackeray's *Vanity Fair*, we read that "the Captain, blushing in a very hurried and discomfited manner, turned away his head."

sage: adj. or n., SAJE, rhymes with *rage*

The adjective or noun **sage** refers to a profoundly wise person. In *The Prince and the Pauper*, Mark Twain wrote that "the sages of the realm ceased from their deliberations." In Christopher Marlowe's *Doctor Faustus*, we read, "Come German Valdes and Cornelius, and make me blest with your sage conference."

plausible: adj., PLOZZ-ih-bull, rhymes with *probable*

The adjective **plausible** refers to something that seems believable, reasonable, or possible. In Marjorie Kinnan Rawlings's *The Yearling*, "Jody had invented a plausible tale of rats on the roof, but his mother was skeptical." Mary Wollstonecraft, in *Vindication of the Rights of Woman*, wrote that "his eloquence renders absurdities plausible."

animated: adj., ANN-ih-mate-ed, rhymes with *laminated*

The adjective **animated** means lively. The verb form is *animate*, and the noun form is *animation*. In *Wuthering Heights*, Emily Brontë wrote that "he looked better when he was animated; that is his everyday countenance." In George Orwell's *1984*, we read that "his face had suddenly become both stern and animated."

obtrude: v., ob-TROOD, rhymes with *unglued*

The verb **obtrude** means to intrude, to become noticeable in an unfortunate manner. The adjective form is *obtrusive*, and its antonym is *unobtrusive*. In Henry David Thoreau's *Walden*, we read, "I should not obtrude my affairs so much on the notice of my readers if very particular inquiries had not been made by my townsmen concerning my mode of life...." In *The Great Gatsby*, F. Scott Fitzgerald wrote that "Sometimes she and Miss Baker talked at once, unobtrusively and with a bantering inconsequence that was never quite chatter."

Henry David Thoreau

The ability to read academic nonfiction is one of the most important elements of academic success. For practice, here is a short nonfiction essay that contains many of the classic words of this lesson.

A friend of the transcendental poet and essayist Ralph Waldo Emerson, Henry David Thoreau achieved a singular place in American letters, not by writing novels or conventional history, but by ethical reflection in his essay *Civil Disobedience,* which later affected both Mahatma Gandhi and Martin Luther King, Jr., and by going to the woods of Walden Pond to live alone and then documenting his reflections on the experience in the vivid journal *Walden, or Life in the Woods.* Thoreau is America's profound sage.

In *Walden,* Thoreau expostulated eloquently against the noisy business of the world that obtrudes itself into one's consciousness, filling the mind with odious distractions and with popular but vulgar and implausible notions. At Walden Pond, Thoreau became a patron of the wildlife, of the woods, and of the serenity of the lake. He venerated the unique individual and the exercise of personal freedom in choosing the commitments of one's own life, without allowing others' preferences to intervene in one's decisions. He was wont to take long walks far from the clamor and din of Concord, the Massachusetts town that lay scarcely a mile from the pond.

Never diffident about his opinions, Thoreau deprecated the mercenary hypocrisies and grotesque, material motivations that led most of his fellow citizens to violate their deepest philosophical and religious principles and to miss the myriad opportunities life offers. He entreated his readers not to cut expedient corners in life in listless languor but to devote their attentions to the sublime decorum of nature, which he viewed as the very visage of God.

The citizens of Concord were perplexed and even discomfited by Thoreau, by his preference for solitude and his prodigious indifference to their expectations. Unabashed, he continued his personal study of the wooded lake, manifesting by his personal example and his fastidious writing that a different life is possible.

Q: What seems to be special about Thoreau?

Inspector of Snow-Storms

Michael Clay Thompson

For many years I was self-appointed inspector
of snow-storms and rain-storms and did my duty
faithfully. – Henry David Thoreau, *Walden*

The day dawned cold; I woke
to find the sky a loud blue, spotless,
serene, the sky implausible, too blue,   adj., adj.
obtruding itself above the white-cloak earth,   adj.
white croakless lake, white shrouds on vivid oaks.   adj.
The day dawned cold; the vexed joke-squirrel   adj.
with tiny pokes of breath gesticulating madly   adj.
in the ferris-tree, running routes fastidiously,   adv.
and cold day animated with red-rogue fox tracks   adj.
and coded mouse tracks and jovial bug crowds in the cold day.   adj.
In the wood, a broken branch cracked, provoked.
Far in the plowed field somewhere, an odious engine   adj.
hacked its haggard cough into the folk sky,   adj.
billows of smoke, like slow-ascending baseballs,   n.
but I, the uncowed patron of the wild stock of the town,   n.
could not intervene. And anyway I had more   v.
subtle work to do, in the cold day, beneath the blue   adj.
and martial visage of the sky. Somewhere back   adj., n.
in the green pine mystery, a wistful fox bark discomfited   adj. v.
a short-term mouse, and the great-browed Sage of the   n.
universe peered down, benevolent, His perfect visage blue   adj., n.
in the cold dawn, a subtle purple portent   adj., n.
still eddying on the hills, waiting for the sun   adj.
to invoke the tremulous world.   adj.

I obeyed, with all my loyalty, the exquisite decorum   adj., n.
of the wild, and I was silent, and stepped respectfully,
in the baroque white of the cold blue dawn.

Classic Words Challenge

In each case below, one of the choices was the word used by the author. Your challenge is to guess which word the author used. This is not a test; it is a game because more than one word choice may work perfectly well. Use your sensitivity and intuition to guess which word the author used. You may need a dictionary.

1. From Jane Austen's *Pride and Prejudice*

   By last summer he was again most painfully ________ on my notice.
   a. discomfited
   b. obtruded
   c. intervened
   d. gesticulated

2. From Mary Shelley's *Frankenstein*

   You have been tutored and refined by books and retirement from the world, and you are, therefore, somewhat ________________.
   a. obsequious
   b. haggard
   c. plausible
   d. fastidious

3. From Charles Dickens's *David Copperfield*

   It was Traddles, whom Mr. Mell instantly ___________ by bidding him hold his tongue.
   a. gesticulated
   b. discomfited
   c. acquiesced
   d. obtruded

4. From William Makepeace Thackeray's *Vanity Fair*

   Osborne came into the coffee-room, looking ________ and pale.
   a. haggard
   b. plausible
   c. impassive
   d. obsequious

Classic Grammar • Parts of Speech

Every vocabulary word is a part of speech, and every sentence is made of vocabulary. To use vocabulary correctly, we must use it grammatically. Many words can be used in several ways.

In the sentences below, you will find our classic vocabulary words, but they may be present as a different part of speech. In other words, you may see a classic adjective we know but in its adverb form or noun form. Think flexibly. On the lines below sentences three through seven, write the part of speech of each word.

1.   I   would   not   be   so   **fastidious**   as   you   are. (Austen)

   pron.   v.   adv.   v.   adv.   adj.   conj.   pron.   v.

---

2.   The   frightened   mother   became   weak   and   **obsequious**. (Wilder)

   adj.   adj.   n.   v.   adj.   conj.   adj.

---

3.   He   **gesticulated**   and   almost   danced   with   excitement. (Doyle)

   pron.   v.   conj.   adv.   v.   prep.   n.

---

4.   Be   a   scholar   and   **sage**   among   the   wisest.... (Hawthorne)

   v.   adj.   n.   conj.   n.   prep.   adj.   n.

---

5.   Ethan   smiled   at   the   **discomfiture**   he   had   caused. (Wharton)

   n.   v.   prep. adj.   n.   pron.   v.   v.

---

6.   I've   told   a   **plausible**   lie   at   the   club. (Conrad)

   pron./v.   v.   adj.   adj.   n.   prep.   adj.   n.

---

7.   It   is   very   **unobtrusive**   in   its   manifestations. (C. Brontë)

   pron.   v.   adv.   adj.   prep.   adj.   n.

Classic Word Muddles

In most of the sentences below, one of the classic words is misused, which means that it is a part of speech error. Can you explain the vocabulary/grammar errors? Some of the sentences contain no errors.

1. The awkward reply was a major **discomfit**.   not a n.
2. He **saged** the group until they apprehended the issue.   not a word
3. The explanation was a complete **plausible**.   not a n.
4. We looked carefully at his **visage** face.   not an adj.
5. The governor had an **ignominy** reputation.   not an adj.
6. He took **fastidious** care of the museum's artifacts.   correct
7. The policy was an odious **obtrude** in our lives.   not a n.
8. The confusion required an **intervene** from the mayor.   not a n.
9. We were appalled by his **odious** discourtesy.   correct
10. He had a **gesticulate** reaction to the interruption.   not an adj.

Classic Centuries: *discomfit*

Below are examples of how *discomfit* has been used through the centuries. Which is your favorite?

1911   Edith Wharton, *Ethan Frome*
        "Ethan smiled at the discomfiture he had caused."
1911   Frances Hodgson Burnett, *The Secret Garden*
        "Mrs. Medlock looked rather discomfited by her apparent indifference."
1895   Thomas Hardy, *Jude the Obscure*
        "Jude looked discomfited."
1854   Charles Dickens, *Hard Times*
        "Mr. Gradgrind was extremely discomfited by this unexpected question."
1847   William Makepeace Thackeray, *Vanity Fair*
        "George only laughed the more at her piteous and discomfited mien."
1594   William Shakespeare, *The Taming of the Shrew*
        "Go with me and be not so discomfited."
1385   Geoffrey Chaucer, *The Canterbury Tales*
        "The pilours diden bisinesse and cure / After the bataille and discomfiture."

An Impression, Influenced by Henry David Thoreau's *Walden*

In the story below, most of the classic words are used well, but one is not. It may be the meaning that is wrong, or it may be the grammar/usage. Please circle the classic word that is not used correctly.

I went to the woods to shed my soul of the obsequious and ignominious compromises of daily society and to know, firsthand, the sage words of nature. I wanted to increase my apprehension of the world's secrets, to hear the plausible whisperings of the wind, to look directly at the placid visage of the lake, and to leave behind the vulgar and odious din of the town, those obtrusive and vexing rules that leave the indolent soul haggard and impassive, without the vivid spirit that should animate it.

I wanted to find the peace necessary for great reading, to read fastidiously and heroically, to absorb the subtle eddies of thought that reside in the classics, those books that extend their eloquence into the profound questions of life. I wanted to read with a martial spirit, a resolute spirit, accepting the challenges of great books and great thinking.

I wanted to live free of languor, to leave behind all pensive diffidence, and to stand forthright in the bracing air, to face the woods with an ostentatious heart, and to avoid the grotesque expedients that make us wince, abashed at the myriad experiences that we miss when we avoid the difficulties of life.

I wanted to supervise the wild stock of the town, to inspect the snow-storms and rain-storms, and to study the exquisite footnotes left by animals in the snow. I wanted to translate the clamor of the discomfited owl, to throw shadows in the moonlight, and to venerate the green shoots and roots growing silently under the pall of snow.

I wanted to importune my spirit to live, to entreat my willingness to endure, and to reprove all forms of despondence and dejection, replacing those defeats with a jovial intention, laughing in grateful acceptance at the blessings conferred upon me by the great Benefactor, rather than living as an **impassive**.

I went to the woods to live and to avoid having to say that I had not lived. I wanted to discover the great secret decorum that organizes life in its different and perplexing forms, including myself. For these reasons, I went to the woods.

Classic Words Character

Let us use some of the words that we are learning. Pretend that you are writing a novel, and write a short description of a character, using some of the words in this lesson. Here is an example:

James gesticulated obsequiously, feigning a deference that he did not really feel. Stooping in haggard disarray, he groped for plausible words to conceal the reason for his visit. His visage communicated his acquiescence to the hotel policy, which he regarded as an odious obtrusion in his personal business, and his hemming and hawing began to discomfit everyone.

Classic Words Place

Now write a short description of a place, a landscape, or a scene, using some of the words in this lesson. Here is an example:

The bleak landscape wore a cloak of hard ice. The trees bent obsequiously down toward the hard ground. Every creature and plant was forced into a silent acquiescence, and the land itself was like a great white visage, staring upward into the blue sky.

Classic Words Invention

Finally, write a short description of something or someone that you imagine, using some of the words in this lesson. Here is an example:

The haggard explorer burst into the room, his usual fastidious appearance transformed into a torn and dusty caricature. He uttered a vulgar oath as he looked around. The discomfited customers stared, commented on the odious look of fear in his visage, and began an animated dialogue about what to do.

RECREATION OF
HENRY DAVID
THOREAU'S CABIN

RACHEL CARSON

Classic Words – Lesson VII

Ten New Words

meditate: to think deeply

oppress: to tyrannize

apparition: a specter

poignant: touching, sad

impute: attribute to

sojourn: a visit

fortnight: a two-week period

intelligible: understandable

mitigate: alleviate

ardor: enthusiasm, passion

Ten Review Words

Caesar's English I

articulate: express clearly

austere: bare

furtive: stealthy

genial: kind

lurid: sensational

Caesar's English II

verdure: vegetation

equivocal: ambiguous

orthodox: traditional

profane: irreverent

tumult: disturbance

meditate: v., MED-ih-tate, rhymes with *contemplate*

The verb **meditate** means to think deeply, quietly, to engage in careful reflection. The noun form is *meditation*, the adjective form is *meditative*, and the adverb form is *meditatively*. In *The Invisible Man*, H.G. Wells wrote that "His meditation became profound." In *Billy Budd*, Herman Melville described "a settled meditative and melancholy expression." In Charles Dickens's *David Copperfield*, we read, "I sat down in a great chair upon the hearth to meditate on my happiness."

oppress: v., oh-PRESS, rhymes with *duress*

To **oppress** is to keep people in a subservient position, to tyrannize them. It also can refer to feelings of anxiety or distress. The noun form is *oppression*, and the adjective is *oppressive*. In *Robinson Crusoe*, Daniel Defoe wrote that "These reflections oppressed me for the second or third day of my distemper." In Jack London's *The Call of the Wild*, we read that "he felt oppressed by the vague sense of impending calamity."

apparition: n., ah-par-ISH-un, rhymes with *nutrition*

The noun **apparition** refers to a ghost or a ghostlike appearance, a specter. In *The Hound of the Baskervilles*, Arthur Conan Doyle wrote that "she was, indeed, a strange apparition upon a lonely moorland path."

poignant: adj., POIN-yent, rhymes with *brilliant*

The adjective **poignant** refers to something that causes a sense of sadness or regret. It also can refer to a sharp smell or taste. The noun form is *poignancy*. In Bram Stoker's *Dracula*, we read that "He shook his head sadly, and with a look of poignant regret on his face."

impute: v., im-PYOOT, rhymes with *dispute*

The verb **impute** means to attribute something, possibly but not necessarily something discreditable, to someone else. The noun form is *imputation*. In Jonathan Swift's *Gulliver's Travels*, we read that "none would complain of broken promises, but impute their disappointments wholly to fortune." In *Pride and Prejudice*, Jane Austen wrote that "He generously imputed the whole to his mistaken pride."

sojourn: n. or v., SOH-jern, rhymes with *modern*

The noun or verb **sojourn** refers to a visit, a stay that is only temporary. A person who sojourns is called a sojourner. In *Walden*, Henry David Thoreau wrote that "At present I am a sojourner in civilized life again." In Harper Lee's *To Kill a Mockingbird*, we read that "My sojourn in the corner was a short one."

fortnight: n., FORT-nite, rhymes with *downright*

A **fortnight** is two-week period—fourteen nights. In *Frankenstein*, Mary Shelley's pitiful monster says, "In another fortnight I was able to leave my chamber." In Jane Austen's *Emma*, we read, "he will be with us within a fortnight." In *Animal Farm*, George Orwell wrote that "The whole thing would be over in a fortnight."

intelligible: adj., in-TELL-ih-jih-ble, rhymes with *eligible*

The adjective **intelligible** refers to something that is understandable, comprehensible. Its opposite is *unintelligible*. In her *Vindication of the Rights of Woman*, Mary Wollstonecraft wrote that "it is difficult to render intelligible such a ridiculous jargon." Charles Dickens, in *David Copperfield*, described a character "talking about something or other, but not at all intelligibly."

mitigate: v., MIT-ih-gate, rhymes with *irrigate*

The verb **mitigate** means to alleviate, to make less severe or less painful. The noun form is *mitigation*. In *Wuthering Heights*, Emily Brontë wrote that "there was a grace in his manner that mitigated these defects." In Joseph Conrad's *Lord Jim*, we read that "the verdict must have been of unmitigated guilt." In *Song of Solomon*, Toni Morrison wrote, "None of that, however, had mitigated the reluctance of her publishers to bring out her complete collected works."

ardor: n., AHR-dor, rhymes with *armor*

The noun **ardor** refers to enthusiasm, to passion. The adjective form is *ardent*, and the adverb is *ardently*. In Jane Austen's *Pride and Prejudice*, Mr. Darcy says, "You must allow me to tell you how ardently I admire and love you." In his *Narrative*, Frederick Douglass wrote that "I had at one time over forty scholars, and those of the right sort, ardently desiring to learn."

Rachel Carson

The ability to read academic nonfiction is one of the most important elements of academic success. For practice, here is a short nonfiction essay that contains many of the classic words of this lesson.

In the 1950s, toxic insecticides such as DDT pervaded the natural environment in the United States, causing myriad odious effects on fish and wildlife and illnesses in the human population. Today the environment is healthier because many of those pesticides have been banned, and credit goes to one of America's most venerated biologists, Rachel Carson, whose eloquent 1962 book *Silent Spring* alerted Americans to the prodigious damage of insecticides and initiated an environmental clamor that resulted in cleaner air and water. With fastidious precision, Carson vividly detailed the risk of DDT to the Bald Eagle; DDT caused the eagle's eggshells to be so thin that they broke, killing the chicks—a portent of approaching environmental calamity.

DDT is a persistent carcinogen that is harmful to many forms of wildlife, but it is especially damaging to birds. Once sprayed into the environment, it remains inexorably toxic for up to three decades without dissipating, and the impending extinction of many bird species seemed to be a real possibility. After Carson's book, DDT was banned in the entire United States in 1972 and then worldwide by the Stockholm Convention of 2001.

Carson's profound findings on the grotesque effects of pesticides discomfited the chemical pesticide industry, whose sales to farmers amounted to millions of dollars, and they expostulated against her findings and deprecated her competence, objecting to her obtrusion of facts into the profitable status quo, but President Kennedy intervened. He ordered his Science Advisory Committee to study Carson's claims, and the committee found that Carson's study was accurate. The vexed chemical industry was forced to acquiesce to the facts of pesticide pollution.

Carson's landmark science eventually led to the creation of the Environmental Protection Agency, or EPA. In 1980 President Carter awarded Rachel Carson the Presidential Medal of Freedom, the highest civilian honor an American citizen can receive.

Q: What interests you in this essay about Rachel Carson?

"The Rest Is Silence." *Hamlet*, V. ii.

Michael Clay Thompson

The sedge has wither'd from the lake,
  And no birds sing.
    – John Keats, "La Belle Dame Sans Merci"

From the fields, a grotesque, sallow serenity.   adj., adj., n.
No birds sang...where had they gone?
Perplexed and wistful, people asked of birds,   adj., adj.
their plaintive voices feigning sanguine hopefulness.   adj., adj., adj.
The feeding stations in the verdure were deserted,   n.
unworded, where late the sweet bard's sweet birds sang
the song that now had dissipated in the somber, converted wind.   v., adj.
The few birds seen anywhere were listless, furtive;   adj., adj.
with wings tremulous, they could not fly. Disturbing,   adj.
this hush-spring, placid and taciturn, austere.   adj., adj.
On poignant mornings that had once throbbed   adj.
with the genial chorus of rockin' robins, catbirds, doves,   adj.
jovial jays, wrens, and myriads of ardent birdwords,
no sound now mitigated the pensive, inverted null,   v., adj., adj.
the lurid, discomfiting silence, the audible zero.   adj., adj., adj.
No tweet articulated the sweet and inexorable clamor of life;   v., adj., n.
the derisive tumult of spring had abated, deserted, disworded.   adj., n., v.
A prodigious and oppressive pause interposed itself,   adj., adj., v.
a burden, like a wan, morose apparition   adj., adj., n.
over the torpid, unbirded fields   adj.
and obsequious woods and   adj.
marsh.

Tremulous in indolent wind,   adj., adj.
fastidious flowers bloomed   adj.
for no reason.

Classic Words Challenge

In each case below, one of the choices was the word used by the author. Your challenge is to guess which word the author used. This is not a test; it is a game because more than one word choice may work perfectly well. Use your sensitivity and intuition to guess which word the author used. You may need a dictionary.

1. From Edith Wharton's *Ethan Frome*

   These memories came back with the ______________ of vanished things.
      a. fortnight
      b. orthodoxy
      c. poignancy
      d. austerity

2. From Arthur Conan Doyle's *The Hound of the Baskervilles*

   To him it may have been an ______________ relief.
      a. unmitigated
      b. unintelligible
      c. unorthodox
      d. inarticulate

3. From Charles Dickens's *David Copperfield*

   Their gloom and ______________ utterly destroyed her.
      a. oppression
      b. austerity
      c. equivocation
      d. mitigation

4. From Jane Austen's *Emma*

   It was charity to _________ some of her unbecoming indifference to the languor of ill-health.
      a. articulate
      b. profane
      c. meditate
      d. impute

Classic Grammar • Parts of Speech

Every vocabulary word is a part of speech, and every sentence is made of vocabulary. To use vocabulary correctly, we must use it grammatically. Many words can be used in several ways.

In the sentences below, you will find our classic vocabulary words, but they may be present as a different part of speech. In other words, you may see a classic adjective we know but in its adverb form or noun form. Think flexibly. On the lines below sentences three through seven, write the part of speech of each word.

1.   I **ardently** longed to comprehend these also. (M. Shelley)

      pron.   adv.   v.   --------------n.------------   pron.   adv.

2.   I am a **sojourner** in civilized life again. (Thoreau)

      pron. v. adj.   n.   prep.   adj.   n.   adv.

3.   It was about a **fortnight** after the funeral. (Stowe)

      pron. v.   prep. adj.   n.   prep. adj.   n.

4.   The silence at once became intolerably **oppressive**. (Conrad)

      adj.   n.   prep. n.   v.   adv.   adj.

5.   Mozart has an **austere** elegance.... (Hilton)

      n.   v.   adj.   adj.   n.

6.   Your meaning must be **unequivocal**. (Austen)

      adj.   n.   v.   v.   adj.

7.   His voice was hardly **intelligible**. (E. Brontë)

      adj.   n.   v.   adv.   adj.

Classic Word Muddles

In most of the sentences below, one of the classic words is misused, which means that it is a part of speech error. Can you explain the vocabulary/grammar errors? Some of the sentences contain no errors.

1.	He **apparitioned** right in front of us.	not a word
2.	We waited patiently until the **fortnight** time.	not an adj.
3.	The sad event was a complete **poignant**.	not a n.
4.	They were guilty of an **impute** criticism.	not an adj.
5.	His **equivocal** reply was perplexing to us.	correct
6.	We took a **sojourn** trip to the coast of Italy.	not an adj.
7.	I took a week for a long, profound **meditate**.	not a n.
8.	The **mitigate** made a difference in everyone's attitude.	not a n.
9.	Her **ardor** support was welcome in the crisis.	not an adj.
10.	He **imputed** opinions to her that she did not feel.	correct

Classic Centuries: *poignant*

Below are examples of how *poignant* has been used through the centuries. Which is your favorite?

1963   Martin Luther King, Jr., *Why We Can't Wait*
        "It is even more poignant to contemplate the words of this boy."

1927   Thornton Wilder, *The Bridge of San Luis Rey*
        "The distress of remorse was less poignant than the distress of fasting."

1895   Stephen Crane, *The Red Badge of Courage*
        "This was to be a poignant retaliation."

1851   Nathaniel Hawthorne, *The House of the Seven Gables*
        "Clifford's naturally poignant sympathies were all aroused."

1850   Charles Dickens, *David Copperfield*
        "All the shame and misery...became more poignant as I thought of this."

1816   Mary Shelley, *Frankenstein*
        "They often, I believe, suffered the pangs of hunger very poignantly."

1385   Geoffrey Chaucer, *The Canterbury Tales*
        "Of poynaunt sauce hir neded never a deel."

An Impression, Influenced by Rachel Carson's *Silent Spring*

In the story below, most of the classic words are used well, but one is not. It may be the meaning that is wrong, or it may be the grammar/usage. Please circle the classic word that is not used correctly.

In the long development of the phenomenon of animate life on earth, the organisms on our planet settled into a profound ecological balance, a genial balance that benefitted all life. This great natural balance — which included water, air, the earth and minerals, the green verdure, insects, microorganisms, and all animals — was a sustaining harmony, one that would promote the success and endurance of living things on the planet.

But now a singular apparition — silent and invisible — is bringing obtrusive and indiscriminate death into this system. In recent decades the agricultural industries have sprayed hundreds of thousands of tons of odious toxic chemicals, such as DDT, into this hitherto balanced environment. The purpose of the chemicals is to control or kill organisms that feed upon our crops, but the chemicals have acute poisonous and grotesque effects far beyond their intended purpose. They are, in fact, not just insecticides but biocides. They kill virtually all life — not just the so-called harmful insects but a myriad of insects, as well as the birds and frogs and other animals that feed on them.

The pesticide industry's orthodox **feign** defense of these insecticides is that they help us feed our population, bringing the benefits of good nutrition to the country. This may sound plausible, but the poignant truth is that these chemicals have the dangerous property of being persistent. Time does not mitigate their toxic effects; they do not dissipate into harmless chemicals but persist even for decades as inexorable poisons. Once sprayed into the environment to control insects, they find their way into the fields and streams, into the bodies of the furtive creatures of the forest, and even into the bodies of human beings, where they continue to accumulate as more and more of the toxic chemicals are ingested.

It is essential for us to confront the facts of the damage that pesticides are doing to our environment and our ecology. We cannot be sanguine or complacent in the face of such risks. We must intervene; we must be resolute and clamor for changes in policy that will stop the prodigious flow of pesticides into our environment.

Classic Words Character

Let us use some of the words that we are learning. Pretend that you are writing a novel, and write a short description of a character, using some of the words in this lesson. Here is an example:

Every fortnight, the apparition appeared at the top of the hill, gesticulating poignantly in the moonlight as though searching for someone. The dim figure appeared to be on a sojourn, moving furtively among the stones, dressed in an austere cloak, and fading back into the dark verdure at the first approach of a human being.

Classic Words Place

Now write a short description of a place, a landscape, or a scene, using some of the words in this lesson. Here is an example:

On the austere tundra, arctic birds articulated the cryptic language of the North. Small mammals scurried in furtive movements between the rocks. Somewhere in the distance, a polar bear captured its lunch in a tumult of sudden aggression. Soon, the winter wind would begin to drive the land flat, streaming over the ground with freezing ardor.

Classic Words Invention

Finally, write a short description of something or someone that you imagine, using some of the words in this lesson. Here is an example:

His genial visage did not mitigate the resentment she felt for his equivocal approach to the help she had requested. A number of profane and even vulgar replies occurred to her, but she chose instead to issue an orthodox courtesy—some standard language. She would find the time, later, to articulate her feelings in a way that even he could understand.

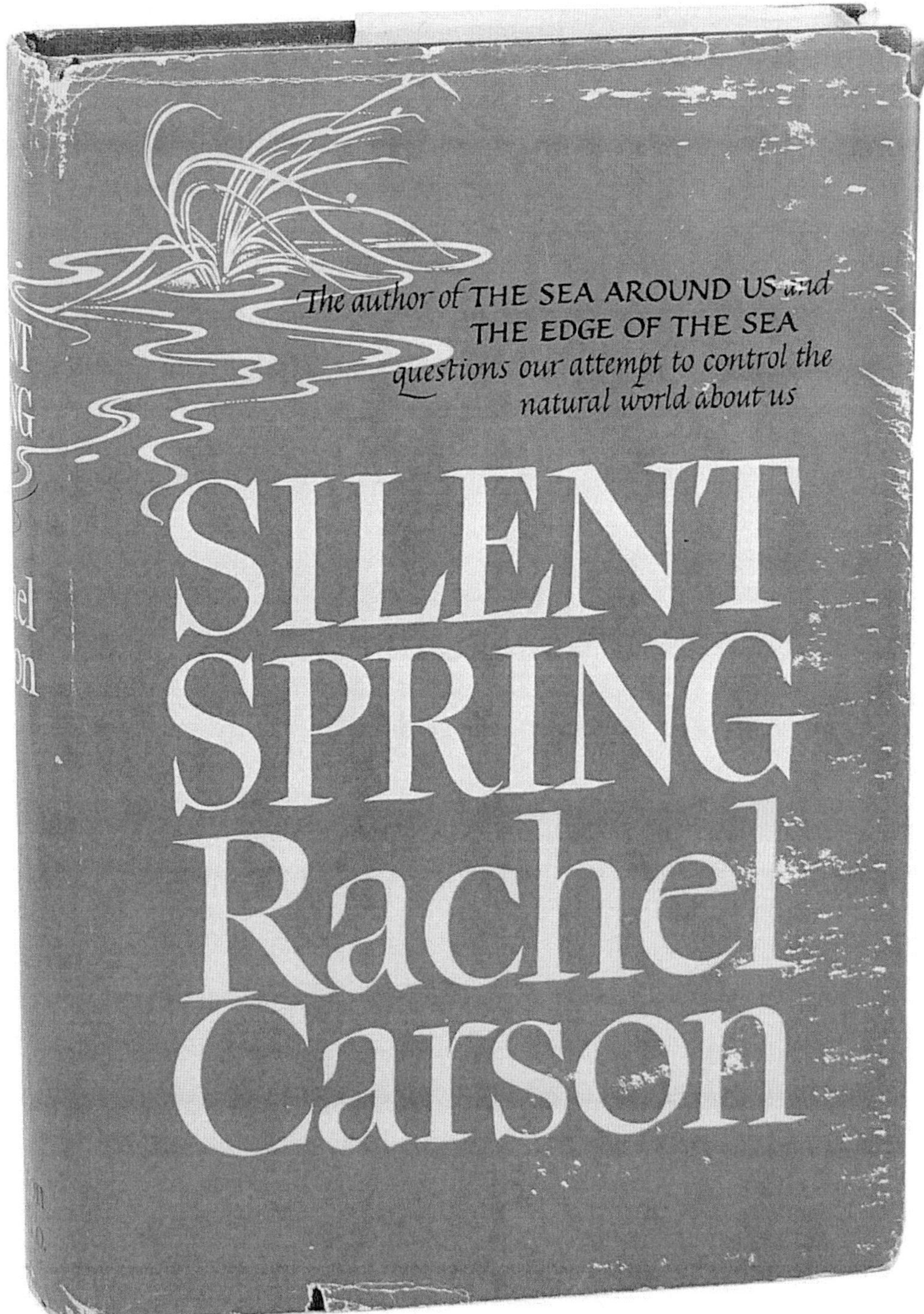

The author of THE SEA AROUND US and THE EDGE OF THE SEA questions our attempt to control the natural world about us
SILENT SPRING
Rachel Carson

MARK TWAIN

Classic Words – Lesson VIII

Ten New Words

semblance: appearance

requite: to repay

congenial: agreeable

indefatigable: tireless

anecdote: a short account

ponder: to consider carefully

suffuse: to spread over

physiognomy: facial features

pertinacity: stubborn persistence

assiduous: diligent

Ten Review Words

Caesar's English I

palpable: touchable

pervade: spread throughout

pallor: paleness

abyss: bottomless depth

martyr: one who suffers

Caesar's English II

incongruous: incompatible

malevolence: ill will

ambiguous: uncertain

felicity: great happiness

irrevocable: unalterable

semblance: n., SEM-blence, rhymes with *dependence*

The noun **semblance** refers to the outward appearance that sometimes but not always conceals a different inner reality, like a mask or facade. In *Kidnapped*, Robert Louis Stevenson wrote, "nor was there any semblance of a garden." In Bram Stoker's *Dracula*, we read, "What manner of man is this, or what manner of creature is it in the semblance of man?" In *1984*, George Orwell wrote that "perhaps it was only a memory taking on the semblance of sound."

requite: v., reh-KWITE, rhymes with *tonight*

To **requite** is to pay back, to return in kind. The adjective form is *requited*, and the negative of that is *unrequited*. In *The Scarlet Letter*, Nathaniel Hawthorne wrote that "Pearl felt the sentiment, and requited it with the bitterest hatred." In *Frankenstein*, Mary Shelley's poor monster says, "I had feelings of affection, and they were requited by detestation and scorn."

congenial: adj., kon-JEE-nee-ull, rhymes with *venial*

The adjective **congenial** means agreeable, pleasant, because of an easy similarity of interests or feelings. The noun form is *congeniality*, and the antithesis of the adjective is *uncongenial*. In *Vindication of the Rights of Woman*, Mary Wollstonecraft asked, "Why should they be bitterly censured for seeking a congenial mind?"

indefatigable: adj., in-deh-FAT-ih-ga-bel, rhymes with *immitigable*

The adjective **indefatigable** refers to someone who cannot be fatigued, who is tireless. In Daniel Defoe's *Robinson Crusoe*, we read that "I showed them with what indefatigable pains I had hewed a large tree into single planks." In *Vanity Fair*, William Makepeace Thackeray describes a character as "This indefatigable pursuer of truth."

anecdote: n., ANN-eck-dote, rhymes with *antidote*

The noun **anecdote** refers to a short, interesting story. It sometimes indicates that the story is mere hearsay. The adjective form is *anecdotal*. In Benjamin Franklin's *Autobiography*, he wrote that he "had lived much among people of distinction and knew a thousand anecdotes of them." In Stephen Crane's *The Red Badge of Courage*, we read that "sometimes he interjected anecdotes."

ponder: v., POND-er, rhymes with *squander*

The verb **ponder** means to think carefully, often before deciding something. In Thomas Hardy's *Jude the Obscure*, we read that "She was doubtfully pondering how to treat this too reflective child." In *The Prince and the Pauper*, Mark Twain wrote that "the Ruffler, who listened, pondered, and then decided."

suffuse: v., suh-FUSE, rhymes with *accuse*

The verb **suffuse** means to spread through gradually. In Sir Walter Scott's *Ivanhoe*, we read that "a deep flush of shame suffused his handsome countenance." In Edith Wharton's *Ethan Frome*, she describes "a square of moon-suffused sky." In *The Red Badge of Courage*, Stephen Crane wrote that "His homely face was suffused with a light of love for the army which was to him all things beautiful and powerful."

physiognomy: n., fizz-ee-ON-oh-mee, rhymes with *autonomy*

The noun **physiognomy** refers to the facial features or expression. It can be used to indicate elements of character or personality. In *The American*, Henry James wrote that "His physiognomy denoted great simplicity, a certain amount of brutality, and a probable failure in the past to profit by rare educational advantages." Charlotte Brontë, in *Jane Eyre*, described how a character's shape "harmonised in squareness with his physiognomy."

pertinacity: n., per-tin-A-city, rhymes with *tenacity*

The noun **pertinacity** refers to firmness in holding to an opinion or an action. The adjective form is *pertinacious*. In *Walden*, Henry David Thoreau described a battle between ants: "They fought with more pertinacity than bulldogs." In *Frankenstein*, Mary Shelley wrote about "the pertinacity with which I continually recurred to the same subject."

assiduous: adj., a-SID-u-us, rhymes with *deciduous*

The adjective **assiduous** means persevering, diligent. The noun form is *assiduity*, and the adverb is *assiduously*. In Benjamin Franklin's *Autobiography*, we read that "He was very pious, an assiduous attendant at the sermons of the best preachers." In *Pride and Prejudice*, Jane Austen wrote that "in your heart, you thoroughly despised the persons who so assiduously courted you."

Mark Twain

The ability to read academic nonfiction is one of the most important elements of academic success. For practice, here is a short nonfiction essay that contains many of the classic words of this lesson.

Samuel Langhorne Clemens, whom we know as Mark Twain, was an indefatigable American writer of poems, essays, short stories, and novels. Twain's novels were charming and humorous, with the rich feeling of extended anecdotes about congenial and eccentric characters who are drawn so completely as to have a semblance of reality. Even his malevolent villains are complex and human—even likeable. His delight in the foibles of these characters is palpable.

Twain's stories are pervaded with voices and details, which he drew from his extraordinary life experiences. In his early years, he served as a printer's apprentice, a typesetter, a printer, a steamboat pilot, a Confederate soldier, a gold miner, and a newspaper reporter. He took a stage coach across the country to Salt Lake City. In these experiences, he absorbed the life and sound of the vast country, and these memories filled his stories with interest.

Twain is best known for his novels *Tom Sawyer* and especially *Huckleberry Finn*, which has been called the Great American Novel because it was the first major novel to establish an authentic American dialect in the narrative voice. Narrated by Huckleberry himself, the novel employs a full range of colloquial vocabulary and bad grammar and tells the story of two steadfast friends—Huck and an escaped slave named Jim—who float down the Mississippi River on a raft. The story is suffused with the incongruous contrast between the profound, tolerant friendship of Huck and Jim and the pervasive intolerance of the greater society.

Twain's assiduous writing produced many popular works, and his efforts were requited with a great deal of money, but he invested his wealth unwisely and was forced to declare bankruptcy. Despite the legal protection of bankruptcy, he insisted on paying all of his creditors in full. In order to repay his creditors, he conducted an extended speaking tour and restored his financial status.

Today, Mark Twain is regarded as the great American novelist and the inventor of the modern novel.

Q: What about Mark Twain's life most interests you?

You Don't Know about Me

Michael Clay Thompson

<table>
<tr><td>

You don't know about me
without you read *Tom Sawyer*
by Mark Twain. He told the truth, mainly,
but there was some stretchers
that **pervaded** his **anecdotes**
of **incongruous** and **ambiguous** situations
and **irrevocable** mistakes,
and his story got **pallid** in places,
but it was the truth mostly.

</td><td>

v., n.
adj., adj.
adj.
adj.

</td></tr>
</table>

You don't know about me
without you **pondered** them tall tales   v.
that stretched the truth mostly.
But it ain't no matter 'cause
you don't know about me
without you read that **abyss** of   n.
stretchers that suffuse that book.
And I ain't **malevolent** towards none,   adj.
and you don't know about me.

You don't know about me,
and I ain't no **assiduous** type,   adj.
and I ain't no **indefatigable**   adj.
workin' **martyr**. I'd rather live slow   n.
on a raft, and just float down the river
with a **congenial** pal, and take in the river,   adj.
and see a steamboat in the dark,
and see them sparks rain down on the river,
and let the steamboat wake joggle the raft,
but you don't know about me
without you read *Tom Sawyer*.

Classic Words Challenge

In each case below, one of the choices was the word used by the author. Your challenge is to guess which word the author used. This is not a test; it is a game because more than one word choice may work perfectly well. Use your sensitivity and intuition to guess which word the author used. You may need a dictionary.

1. From George Eliot's *Silas Marner*

   He saw him continually in some ____________ haunt.
      a. assiduous
      b. congenial
      c. irrevocable
      d. indefatigable

2. From Thomas Hardy's *The Return of the Native*

   To make up for lost time he studied ____________.
      a. malevolently
      b. incongruously
      c. congenially
      d. indefatigably

3. From Charles Dickens's *David Copperfield*

   Mr. Micawber was plying his pen with great ____________.
      a. physiognomy
      b. semblance
      c. assiduity
      d. malevolence

4. From Joseph Conrad's *Lord Jim*

   A marvelous stillness ____________ the world.
      a. pervaded
      b. pondered
      c. suffused
      d. requited

Classic Grammar • Parts of Speech

Every vocabulary word is a part of speech, and every sentence is made of vocabulary. To use vocabulary correctly, we must use it grammatically. Many words can be used in several ways.

In the sentences below, you will find our classic vocabulary words, but they may be present as a different part of speech. In other words, you may see a classic adjective we know but in its adverb form or noun form. Think flexibly. On the lines below sentences three through seven, write the part of speech of each word.

1. His   face   turned   to   a   **semblance**   of   gray   paste. (Crane)

    adj.   n.   v.   prep. adj.   n.   prep. adj.   n.

____

2. I   shall   remember   and   **requite**. (Twain)

    pron. v.   v.   conj.   v.

____

3. He   had   a   **congenial**   task   before   him. (Conan Doyle)

    pron. v. adj.   adj.   n.   prep.   pron.

____

4. The **indefatigable** bell now sounded for the fourth time. (C. Brontë)

    adj.   adj.   n. adv.   v.   prep. adj. adj.   n.

____

5. He   kept   it   between   his   teeth   so   **pertinaciously**. (Dickens)

    pron. v. pron.   prep.   adj. n.   adv.   adv.

____

6. I   am   **irrevocably**   doomed. (Hawthorne)

    pron. v.   adv.   adj.

____

7. The   **suffused**   look   had   gone   from   his   face. (Stoker)

    adj.   adj.   n.   v.   v.   prep. adj.   n.

____

Classic Word Muddles

In most of the sentences below, one of the classic words is misused, which means that it is a part of speech error. Can you explain the vocabulary/grammar errors? Some of the sentences contain no errors.

1.	He is lazy and needs to **assiduous** harder.	not a v.
2.	The amiable fellow was a true **congenial**.	not a n.
3.	You are in my debt and owe me a complete **requite**.	not a n.
4.	We were appalled by his **malevolence** attitude.	not an adj.
5.	She sat thoughtfully under a tree and had a long **ponder**.	not a n.
6.	She was **indefatigable** in her efforts to feed the poor.	correct
7.	He seemed to **semblance** a friend of mine.	*semblance* is a n.
8.	She told a long, disjointed, **anecdote** story.	not an adj.
9.	The result was a baffling **ambiguous**.	not a n.
10.	His illness gave him a **pallor** complexion.	not an adj.

Classic Centuries: *pertinacity*

Below are examples of how *pertinacity* has been used through the centuries. Which is your favorite?

1925   Virginia Wolfe, *Mrs. Dalloway*
        "Hugh was pertinacious."

1903   Jack London, *The Call of the Wild*
        "But in the end Buck's pertinacity was rewarded."

1900   Joseph Conrad, *Lord Jim*
        "There may be those who could have laughed at his pertinacity."

1854   Henry David Thoreau, *Walden*
        "They fought with more pertinacity than bulldogs."

1847   Charlotte Brontë, *Jane Eyre*
        "Why do you remain pertinaciously perched on my knee?"

1820   Washington Irving, *The Legend of Sleepy Hollow*
        "There was something in the moody and dogged silence of this pertinacious companion, that was mysterious and appalling."

1816   Jane Austen, *Emma*
        "The pertinacity of her friend seemed more than she could bear."

An Impression, Influenced by Mark Twain's *Tom Sawyer*

In the story below, most of the classic words are used well, but one is not. It may be the meaning that is wrong, or it may be the grammar/usage. Please circle the classic word that is not used correctly.

The austere Aunt Polly stood still, pondering, listening for that boy, her nephew Tom. Where could he be? Tom was a clever, congenial little fellow, but he was indefatigable in his relentless pursuit of misbehavior. Slowly, an idea began to suffuse her countenance, and she walked over to the closet, opening it with a whish.

There he was, his face covered with jam. She had warned him pertinaciously to stay out of the jam, but he was just as assiduous in getting into it at every opportunity. She stared incredulously at the guilty boy, his pallid physiognomy covered with jam, and she considered how to requite him for this disobedience. He was not malevolent—she knew that—and he had brought much felicity into her life since he came to live with her. His sense of mischief was palpable, and life with him was like living in the midst of an endless anecdote.

Trying to placate her, the boy feigned a semblance of remorse, but Aunt Polly knew that he was not really sorry. There was an incongruous twinkle in his eye that gave him away. There was no ambiguity in the situation; he was a guilty boy who had gotten into the jam once again, despite her sternest warnings, and now some form of punishment was irrevocable. She thought pensively that she would have to be as good as her word if she was to ensure his better behavior in the future.

She reached for the switch that she kept in the house for just such moments as this. A sense of high justice began to pervade her feelings, and her last particle of **poignant** began to dim as she raised the switch to deliver the punishment to the now-despondent-looking boy, when all of a sudden he leaped up and pointed out the window. "Look, Aunt!" he said. "What's that?"

In the split second that it took her to glance out the window, Tom was gone, dashing through the room and out the door into freedom. The fastidious Aunt Polly could only smile like an amiable benefactor at the boy's vivid intelligence. Tom was, in truth, a cute and vivacious boy who meant no harm, and this mitigated against a severe punishment. Outside, she heard a new clamor...what was he up to now?

Classic Words Character

Let us use some of the words that we are learning. Pretend that you are writing a novel, and write a short description of a character, using some of the words in this lesson. Here is an example:

> The boy was indefatigable in his trouble-making. He was not malevolent, but in his congenial way, he broke every rule and caused every grown-up to wince at his playful disobedience. For him, every rule was ambiguous, and every situation offered hidden felicities that only a boy would understand. He strode through the neighborhood, planning schemes with a pertinacity that only another child would truly appreciate.

Classic Words Place

Now write a short description of a place, a landscape, or a scene, using some of the words in this lesson. Here is an example:

> Across the moor, small hills rose above the meager verdure, like upward-turned faces, the physiognomies of the land. The moor seemed to ponder the necessity of its own existence, and the wind communicated a palpable sense of its irrevocable effect, bringing a silence and a chill to the hills.

Classic Words Invention

Finally, write a short description of something or someone that you imagine, using some of the words in this lesson. Here is an example:

> The tall glass of ginger ale was suffused with congenial bubbles, as though the bubble spirit had worked assiduously to fill every space of it. Looking straight down into the glass, one had the feeling of an abyss of soda, a profound and even bottomless depth of bubbles.

MARK TWAIN'S HOUSE

CHARLES DICKENS

Classic Words – Lesson IX

Ten New Words

enmity: hostility

enumerate: to list

sundry: various

vestige: a trace

opaque: not transparent

disconsolate: inconsolable

luminous: light-emitting

effusion: an outpouring

affront: an insult

impediment: an obstruction

Ten Review Words

Caesar's English I

tedious: boring

tangible: touchable

traverse: to cross

repose: resting

undulate: to wave

Caesar's English II

imperious: overbearing

eccentric: unconventional

abject: miserable

adjacent: adjoining

censure: strong criticism

enmity: n., EN-mih-tee, rhymes with *indemnity*

The noun **enmity** refers to active hostility, to deep hatred. In *The Last of the Mohicans*, James Fenimore Cooper wrote that "On Hawkeye he cast a glance of respectful enmity." In Robert Louis Stevenson's *Kidnapped*, we read, "There was now no doubt about my uncle's enmity." In *White Fang*, Jack London described "the enmity that the domestic dog feels for the wolf."

enumerate: v., ee-NOO-mer-ate, rhymes with *commemorate*

To **enumerate** is to list, to mention things one after another. In Jonathan Swift's *Gulliver's Travels*, Gulliver says, "...I enumerated as many sorts as came into my head." In *Vanity Fair*, William Makepeace Thackeray wrote that "...Raggles continued, in a lamentable tone, an enumeration of his griefs." In Charlotte Brontë's *Jane Eyre*, a character begs, "Spare us the enumeration!"

sundry: adj., SUN-dree, rhymes with *country*

The adjective **sundry** means various, of various kinds. In *Jane Eyre*, Charlotte Brontë wrote that "there were sundry questions about tonnage and poundage." In Emily Brontë's *Wuthering Heights*, we read that "Above the chimney were sundry villainous old guns." In Charles Dickens's *David Copperfield*, "there were sundry immense manuscript Books of Evidence."

vestige: n., VESS-tij, rhymes with *message*

The noun **vestige** refers to a trace, often to a trace of something that no longer exists. In James Fenimore Cooper's *The Last of the Mohicans*, a character has "lost every vestige of humanity in a wish for revenge." In his *Narrative*, Frederick Douglass wrote that "There is a vestige of decency, a sense of shame, that does much to curb and check those outbreaks of atrocious cruelty so commonly enacted."

opaque: adj., oh-PAKE, rhymes with *snowflake*

The adjective **opaque** means not transparent; it refers to a material that we cannot see through. It can refer to language that is not clear, not understandable. In Edith Wharton's *Ethan Frome*, we read that "She had pale opaque eyes which revealed nothing and reflected nothing." In *Walden*, Henry David Thoreau described Walden Pond: "the wind slides over its opaque surface in vain."

disconsolate: adj., dis-KONN-so-lit, rhymes with *affiliate*

The adjective **disconsolate** means deeply unhappy, inconsolable. The adverb form is *disconsolately*. In *Jane Eyre*, Charlotte Brontë described "the disconsolate moan of the wind outside." In *David Copperfield*, Charles Dickens wrote that "she would look so scared and disconsolate."

luminous: adj., LOO-min-us, rhymes with *bituminous*

The adjective **luminous** means light-emitting, bright. In Marjorie Kinnan Rawlings's *The Yearling*, we read that "The weathered gray of the split-rail fence was luminous in the rich spring light." In Arthur Conan Doyle's *The Hound of the Baskervilles*, Holmes tells Watson, "It may be that you are not yourself luminous, but you are a conductor of light."

effusion: n., ee-FYOO-zhun, rhymes with *confusion*

The noun **effusion** refers to an outpouring, to a giving off of something such as light or liquid. It can be used to indicate unrestrained speech or writing. The adjective form is *effusive*. In *Pride and Prejudice*, Jane Austen described how "Her daughters listened in silence to this effusion." Mary Shelley, in *Frankenstein*, wrote that "These visions faded when I perused, for the first time, those poets whose effusions entranced my soul, and lifted it to heaven."

affront: n. or v., a-FRONT, rhymes with *blunt*

The noun or verb **affront** refers to behavior that causes offense or even outrage. The adjective form is *affronted*. In Charles Dickens's *David Copperfield*, we read, "...I felt it quite an affront to be supposed proud." In *Kidnapped*, Robert Louis Stevenson wrote that "I have had to swallow an affront."

impediment: n., im-PED-ih-ment, rhymes with *sediment*

The noun **impediment** refers to an obstruction, to a hindrance, as well to a defect in someone's speech. We sometimes see the more formal plural form *impedimenta*. The verb form is *impede*. In H.G. Wells's *The War of the Worlds*, we read that "The growing crowd...was becoming a serious impediment to their excavations." In *Profiles in Courage*, President Kennedy described "this unmanageable mass of incongruous bills, each an impediment to the other."

Charles Dickens

The ability to read academic nonfiction is one of the most important elements of academic success. For practice, here is a short nonfiction essay that contains many of the classic words of this lesson.

Charles Dickens, perhaps the greatest novelist in English literature, wrote popular novels that transformed his own impoverished and troubled background into luminous stories that explored the dignity and humanity of the English working class. Before Dickens, English novels focused on aristocratic characters.

John Dickens, Charles's father, incurred large debts by living beyond his means, and when Charles was twelve years old, his father was placed in Marshalsea debtors' prison, leaving little vestige of the family's honor. Charles's disconsolate mother joined her husband in the prison. His family felicity shattered, Charles was sent to board with a friend of the family, going to the prison on Sundays to visit with his family. The pressures of the abject situation forced Dickens to quit school and work in a grotesque, rat-infested warehouse, sticking labels on containers of boot blacking—a job so difficult and tedious that it made a lasting mark on his feelings about social reform and left him with an enmity for child labor, injustice, and unfairness, as well as a magnanimous respect for the equality of the English common citizen.

Although Dickens's father was released from debtors' prison after he received a small inheritance and paid his debts, the effect on Charles was lasting and was made more bitter by the fact that his mother wished him to continue working in the odious boot-blacking warehouse. These melancholy experiences, far from being an impediment to Dickens's creativity as a writer, strengthened his benevolence, fueled his luminous imagination, and provided an effusion of vivid details that made his stories feel real. For Dickens, poverty and degradation were not imaginary abstractions; they were tangible realities that he remembered from the darkest days of his own life.

Out of the despondence and pain of his early years, Dickens conjured a myriad of vivid and often eccentric characters who are today more real for good readers than actual people they know, and their stories have inoculated generations of readers against complacency, cruelty, and injustice.

Q: What else would you like to know about Charles Dickens?

They Call Me Mr. Pip

Michael Clay Thompson

It's Pirrip, really—that's my name—
but Pip is what I say, a vestige   n.
of my infant voice. My parents
now repose below the soil. They lie   v.
adjacent to the church, and sundry   adj., adj.
brothers too, and I alone survived,
traversed despondent youth,   v., adj.
and stalked the undulating moors,   adj.
and suffered censures of   n.
my sister, Mrs. Joe Gargery—
no luminous benevolence in her   adj., n.
soul for me, but rather enmity, malevolence,   n., n.
the tedious inconvenience of the burden me,   adj.
the gross affront that my abject existence   n., adj.
brings for her inexorable family rule.   adj.
She took me in, says she—imperiously—   adv.
and "brought me up by hand."
A cruel hand, if so. And Joe,
her husband, is a weak but amiable soul,   adj.
and long could I enumerate his   v.
sundry sympathies, his kindnesses to me.   adj.
"Old Pip, old chap," says he, and grins
and finds me no impediment to life.   n.
My future is opaque to me, no scene serene.   adj., adj.
I see no path congenial to my isolated heart,   adj.
no start, but now a din and there a sojourn,   n., n.
a journey of assiduous toil, a burning   adj.
grimace of hard days without felicity.   n., n.
I fain would know what life will bring,   adv.
but now I languish, listless. I swing   v., adj.
between my somber sister's cruel rebuke   adj.
and good old Joe's obsequious diffidence.   adj., n.

Classic Words Challenge

In each case below, one of the choices was the word used by the author. Your challenge is to guess which word the author used. This is not a test; it is a game because more than one word choice may work perfectly well. Use your sensitivity and intuition to guess which word the author used. You may need a dictionary.

1. From Charles Dickens's *David Copperfield*

   She was mortally ____________ by his marriage.
   a. enumerated
   b. traversed
   c. censured
   d. affronted

2. From H.G. Wells's *The Invisible Man*

   It grew cloudy and __________ even as they stared.
   a. luminous
   b. tangible
   c. opaque
   d. tedious

3. From George Orwell's *1984*

   Most of it was a(n) ____________ routine.
   a. tangible
   b. abject
   c. tedious
   d. eccentric

4. From William Golding's *Lord of the Flies*

   He trotted through the sand, enduring the sun's __________.
   a. effusion
   b. vestige
   c. affront
   d. enmity

Classic Grammar • Parts of Speech

Every vocabulary word is a part of speech, and every sentence is made of vocabulary. To use vocabulary correctly, we must use it grammatically. Many words can be used in several ways.

In the sentences below, you will find our classic vocabulary words, but they may be present as a different part of speech. In other words, you may see a classic adjective we know but in its adverb form or noun form. Think flexibly. On the lines below sentences three through seven, write the part of speech of each word.

1. Here she **enumerated** several commissions at **sundry** shops. (Hardy)

    adv.   pron.   v.   adj.   n.   prep. adj.   n.

2. It was but an **effusion** of lively spirits. (Austen)

    pron.   v.   adv.   adj.   n.   prep.   adj.   n.

3. I have had to swallow an **affront**. (Stevenson)

    pron.   v.   v.   ------------n.------------   adj.   n.

4. The most **abject** of the two victims continued motionless. (Cooper)

    adj.   adv.   adj. prep. adj. adj.   n.   v.   adv.

5. For a time I stood regarding these **vestiges**. (Wells)

    prep.   adj.   n.   pron.   v.   adj.   adj.   n.

6. The **opaque**, mad look came into his eyes again. (Golding)

    adj.   adj.   adj.   n.   v.   prep.   adj.   n.   adv.

7. It was a **tedious** and troublesome piece of work. (Twain)

    pron.   v.   adj.   adj.   conj.   adj.   n.   prep.   n.

Classic Word Muddles

In most of the sentences below, one of the classic words is misused, which means that it is a part of speech error. Can you explain the vocabulary/grammar errors? Some of the sentences contain no errors.

1.	On the horizon, the sun created a **luminous**.	not a n.
2.	There was an **effusion** outburst from the fan.	not an adj.
3.	We tried to **vestige** the history of the group.	*vestige* is a n.
4.	I handed Tom the long **enumerate**.	not a n.
5.	Please do not **impediment** this process.	not a v.
6.	He was an **imperious** and refused to speak.	not a n.
7.	Beside the barn, he wanted to build an **adjacent**.	not a n.
8.	The **tedious** blabbermouth never stopped talking.	correct
9.	Instead of glass, they used an **opaque**.	not a n.
10.	She tried to **disconsolate** her opponent.	*disconsolate* is an adj.

Classic Centuries: *effusion*

Below are examples of how *effusion* has been used through the centuries. Which is your favorite?

1906 Jack London, *White Fang*
"Yet White Fang was never effusively affectionate."

1876 Mark Twain, *Tom Sawyer*
"The prize was delivered to Tom with as much effusion as the superintendent could pump up under the circumstances."

1851 Nathaniel Hawthorne, *The House of the Seven Gables*
"She looked into Clifford's face, and beheld there a soft natural effusion."

1816 Jane Austen, *Emma*
"It was but an effusion of lively spirits."

1813 Jane Austen, *Pride and Prejudice*
"Her daughters listened in silence to this effusion."

1792 Mary Wollstonecraft, *Vindication of the Rights of Woman*
"These were not the ravings of imbecility, the sickly effusions of distempered brains."

1667 John Milton, *Paradise Lost*
"And from about him fierce Effusion roll'd."

An Impression, Influenced by Charles Dickens's *Great Expectations*

In the story below, most of the classic words are used well, but one is not. It may be the meaning that is wrong, or it may be the grammar/usage. Please circle the classic word that is not used correctly.

"Hold your noise!" cried a malevolent voice as a man stood up from among the graves adjacent to the church porch. "Keep still, you little devil, or I'll cut your throat!"

I froze, not wishing to affront the man, some vagabond, eccentric, but then I saw the irons on his leg and knew him for a convict on the run, no vestige of decency left in him, I thought. He crouched, disconsolate, expostulating sundry curses, grabbing for my collar. He turned me upside-down and shook the contents of my pockets on the ground. His desperation was palpable, his **effusion** words frightening.

"Here," he said, "you know what vittles is?"

I did. Food. He wanted food, the starving soul, the abject creature. I told him that I'd bring him food. I meant it. "A file, too," he said, his voice a growl, his haggard countenance a grimace. "A file, to hack these irons from my feet."

The irons were cruel impediments to him. How could he now traverse the freezing, undulating moor, the constables on his trail? How could he seek repose, knowing that the hunt was on to drag him back in chains? His future was opaque—no way to know his fate. It was impossible to enumerate his woes, the poor suffering soul.

"I'll bring you vittles, sir," I begged, entreated, obsequiously indeed.

"You do it, lad," said he, and he seemed to soften his initial enmity. Pain suffused his face; he cringed; he tried to hide his now-grotesque despondence. I sympathized with him. I admit it. I knew I should not help a convict to escape, but now my sympathy increased and did not dissipate. I wanted this morose and hopeless fellow to survive.

"I'll bring you vittles, sir, and a file to free you from your bonds." He looked at me, his sallow face evincing plaintive hope, a trace, and gesticulated softly toward my sister's house on the horizon.

"Yes," he said. "You do it, or I'll see you in your grave tonight."

I knew he did not mean that. How? Don't know. Just knew, and knew that any tangible support I gave the suffering soul would mean a lot to him. I'd be his benefactor, at least for this one day.

Classic Words Character

Let us use some of the words that we are learning. Pretend that you are writing a novel, and write a short description of a character, using some of the words in this lesson. Here is an example:

No vestige remained of Elmer's former imperious attitude. He sat, humble and disconsolate, reviewing his sundry bad decisions, wishing that some luminous person had given him better advice. Now he was just an abject eccentric, writhing in an effusion of discomfiting memories.

Classic Words Place

Now write a short description of a place, a landscape, or a scene, using some of the words in this lesson. Here is an example:

The jungle stretched for miles, covering the undulating hills, the luminous beams of sunlight streaking down from the high tree canopy to the leafy forest floor. An effusion of cries from birds and frogs filled the air, and vines and reptiles were an impediment to all efforts to traverse the thick verdure.

Classic Words Invention

Finally, write a short description of something or someone that you imagine, using some of the words in this lesson. Here is an example:

She had coughed for days. It was a tedious cough, an affront to her healthy lifestyle. She had filled her days with exercise and good food, and now here she was, in involuntary repose, coughing her life away in abject and disconsolate misery. Maybe tomorrow she would feel better.

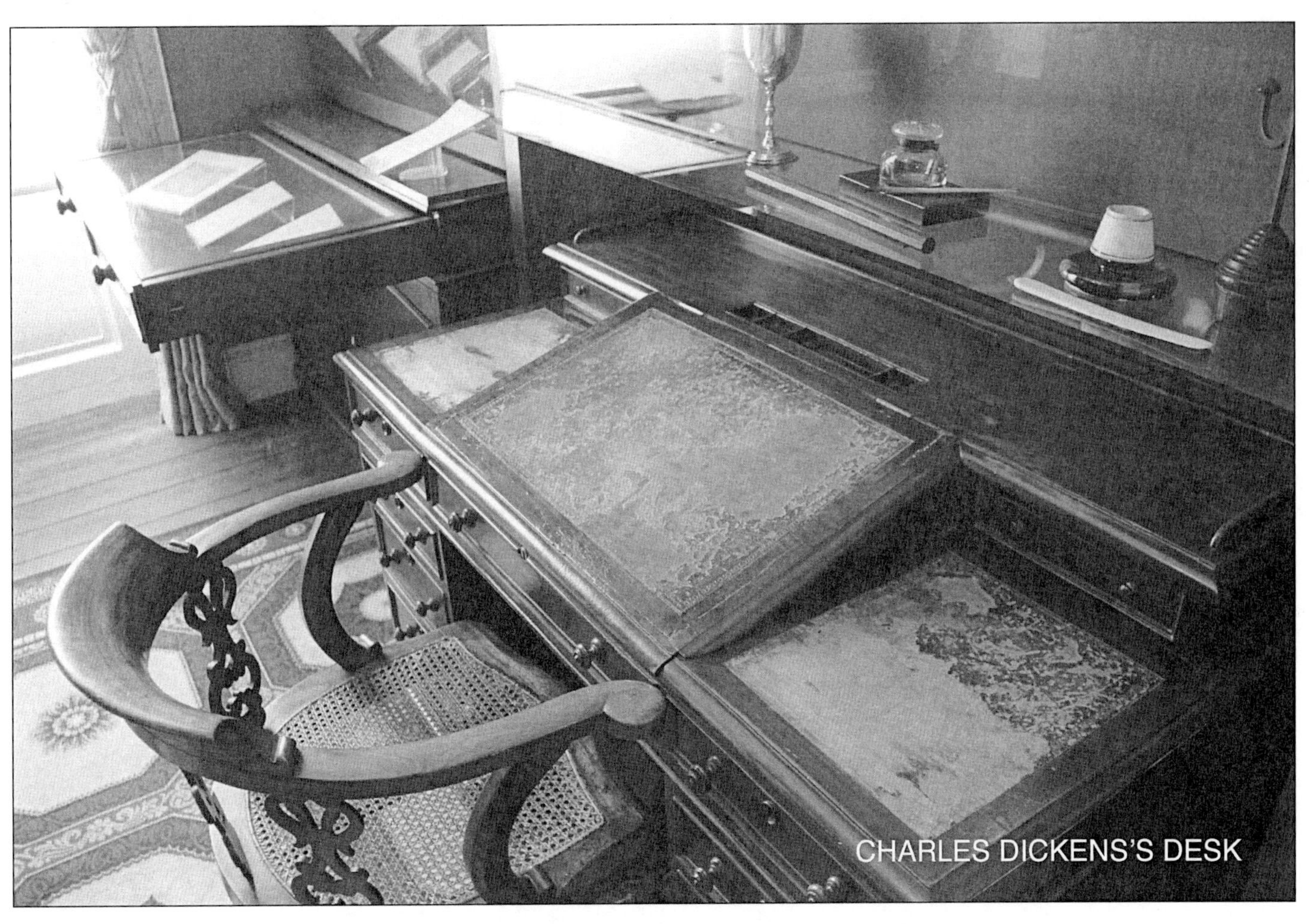

CHARLES DICKENS'S DESK

GEORGE ELIOT

Classic Words – Lesson X

Ten New Words

ruminate: think deeply

accost: to confront

petulant: bad-tempered

efface: erase

edify: to instruct

voluble: speaking incessantly

obeisance: a gesture of respect

ascertain: to make sure

obdurate: refusing to change

antipathy: deep dislike

Ten Review Words

Caesar's English I

prostrate: lying down

remonstrate: to object

stolid: unemotional

superfluous: extra

sagacity: wisdom

Caesar's English II

transient: existing briefly

latent: present but inactive

solicitude: concern

livid: bruised or pale

epithet: a characterizing term

ruminate: v., ROO-min-ate, rhymes with *illuminate*

The verb **ruminate** means to think deeply, with a comparison to a cow chewing its cud. In *David Copperfield*, Charles Dickens wrote that "he bought me a pudding, and having set it before me, seemed to ruminate, and to become absent in his mind for some moments." In Thomas Hardy's *The Return of the Native*, we read, "it was inevitable that she should soon cease to ruminate upon her own condition."

accost: v., a-COST, rhymes with *flossed*

To **accost** is to confront someone, especially by approaching him or her aggressively. In *Wuthering Heights*, Emily Brontë wrote that "it would have been impossible to have accosted him rationally." In Herman Melville's *Moby Dick*, we read that "As he mounted the deck Ahab abruptly accosted him." In H.G. Wells's *The Invisible Man*, a character says, "I was half-minded to accost some passer-by."

petulant: adj., PET-choo-lent, rhymes with *stimulant*

The adjective **petulant** means bad-tempered, sulky in an immature way. The noun form is *petulance*. In *Uncle Tom's Cabin*, Harriet Beecher Stowe's character "threw back her suggestions with a restless petulance." In *The Return of the Native*, Thomas Hardy wrote that "She vented petulant words every now and then."

efface: v., eh-FACE, rhymes with *replace*

To **efface** is to erase from a surface, but it may have a metaphorical meaning, as to efface someone's resentment. To be self-effacing is to diminish oneself. In Charlotte Brontë's *Jane Eyre*, we read that "joy soon effaced every other feeling." In *Ethan Frome*, Edith Wharton wrote that "Zeena answered in a tone of plaintive self-effacement."

edify: v., EDD-ih-fie, rhymes with *modify*

The verb **edify** means to instruct, especially in moral or intellectual matters. The noun form is *edification*, and the adjective form is *edifying* In Charles Dickens's *David Copperfield*, we read that "I was chiefly edified, I am afraid, by the pictures, which were numerous." In *1984*, George Orwell described a character who "sat listening with a sort of gaping solemnity, a sort of edified boredom."

voluble: adj., VOL-yoo-bul, rhymes with *soluble*

The adjective **voluble** means speaking incessantly. The noun form is *volubility*, and the adverb form is *volubly*. In Henry James's *The American*, we read that "She can express displeasure, volubly, in two or three languages." In *Lord Jim*, Joseph Conrad wrote that "He was voluble like a youngster on the eve of a long holiday."

obeisance: n., oh-BEE-sence, rhymes with *malfeasance*

The noun **obeisance** can mean either deferential respect or an actual bow or curtsy. In *Pride and Prejudice*, Jane Austen described the obsequious Mr. Collins "waiting near the lodges, to make them his parting obeisance." In Sir Walter Scott's *Ivanhoe*, we read that the Saxon serfs "made their rude obeisance."

ascertain: v., a-ser-TANE, rhymes with *appertain*

The verb **ascertain** means to make sure, to find out for certain. In *Wuthering Heights*, Emily Brontë described characters who are "anxious to ascertain the truth of her statement." Frederick Douglass, in his *Narrative*, wrote that "I therefore, though with great prudence, commenced early to ascertain their views and feelings in regard to their condition."

obdurate: adj., OB-dure-it, rhymes with *considerate*

The adjective **obdurate** means refusing to change what one is thinking or doing. The adverb form is *obdurately*. In *Paradise Lost*, John Milton described "huge affliction and dismay, / Mixt with obdurate pride and steadfast hate." In *David Copperfield*, Charles Dickens wrote that "a sullen obdurate disposition is, of all tempers, the worst."

antipathy: n., ann-TIH-pah-thee, rhymes with *sympathy*

The noun **antipathy** refers to a deep dislike, an aversion. In *Gulliver's Travels*, Jonathan Swift wrote that "I never beheld in all my travels so disagreeable an animal, nor one against which I naturally conceived so strong an antipathy." In Charlotte Brontë's *Jane Eyre*, we read that "John had not much affection for his mother and sisters, and an antipathy to me."

George Eliot

The ability to read academic nonfiction is one of the most important elements of academic success. For practice, here is a short nonfiction essay that contains many of the classic words of this lesson.

George Eliot was born Mary Ann Evans, but when she became a writer, she changed her name to a male *nom de plume* because she thought female authors were not respected in stolid English literary circles. She did not, however, prostrate herself before this attitude. In fact, she herself had obdurate antipathy for the voluble traditions of romantic stories that many female novelists employed, and she wrote an essay for the *Westminster Review* entitled "Silly Novels by Lady Novelists."

Whatever the status of novels by other authors in Eliot's time, there was nothing silly about her novels, which are among the most profound in English literature. Her novels, such as *Adam Bede*, *Silas Marner*, *The Mill on the Floss*, *Middlemarch*, and *Daniel Deronda*, explore realistic and sagacious themes of small-minded conformists and their persecution and censure of individuality. She created vivid rural settings and deep, complex, eccentric, and often disturbing characters, especially social outsiders. Virginia Woolf articulated it well, saying that Eliot wrote novels for grown-ups.

It is not possible to ascertain every motivation for Eliot's themes, but certainly she experienced some of the rejection and the transient happiness that she portrays in her novels. Her long relationship with the philosopher George Lewes was regarded as scandalous, and when after his death she remarried and went on honeymoon to Italy, her disconsolate—apparently depressed—new husband John Cross leaped from their hotel balcony into a Venice canal. Ironically, he was rescued, but she became ill and died not long after. Her husband, recovering his solicitude in the wake of her death, wrote an eloquent biography of her life, an exaggerated obeisance to her talent that no one took seriously.

During Eliot's life her novels sold well, and even Queen Victoria was an admirer of her work. Today George Eliot has a place in the pantheon of great British writers, alongside Charles Dickens and Jane Austen.

Q: What do you think is most interesting about George Eliot?

I'm Mary, Call Me George

Michael Clay Thompson

The **stolid** souls close ranks.	adj.
They stand like bulls, lock horns,	
and show **antipathy** to all	n.
outsiders. **Sagacious** in their blank	adj.
conformity, and **petulant**, a wall	adj.
of social uniformity. What chance have I	
to gain a place? They would **efface**	v.
all **vestiges**, all trace, of individuality,	n.
expect my cowering **obeisance**. Oh,	n.
I state no reasons though.	
I'm Mary, call me George.	
The **stolid** souls close ranks;	adj.
their **obdurate** insistence warns	adj.
me to stay away, obey, and thank	
you sir and sir and sir for every crumb	
of your **solicitude**, and oh how I am	n.
edified by your **sagacity**, yes sir;	v. (passive voice), n.
I humbly prostrate myself before your	
high importance, yes. What do I seek?	
Nothing unique.	
I'm Mary, call me George.	
The **stolid** souls close ranks,	adj.
and hurl **rebukes** and **epithets** on those	n., n.
whose minds diverge,	
those from the flanks,	
and now I **wince**, **prostrate**, **abashed**,	v., adj., adj.
like one untouchable, unwashed,	
my genius **latent**, never **manifest**,	adj., adj.
a hidden thing and faded, me, **grotesque**.	adj.
I'm Mary, call me George.	

Classic Words Challenge

In each case below, one of the choices was the word used by the author. Your challenge is to guess which word the author used. This is not a test; it is a game because more than one word choice may work perfectly well. Use your sensitivity and intuition to guess which word the author used. You may need a dictionary.

1. From George Eliot's *Silas Marner*

   This excessive _______ and self-questioning is perhaps a morbid habit....
   a. obeisance
   b. rumination
   c. antipathy
   d. solicitude

2. From Mary Shelley's *Frankenstein*

   I had conceived a violent _______ even to the name of natural philosophy.
   a. luminous
   b. tangible
   c. antipathy
   d. tedious

3. From Jane Austen's *Emma*

   You had better look about you, and _____________ what you do....
   a. ascertain
   b. efface
   c. remonstrate
   d. ruminate

4. From Emily Brontë's *Wuthering Heights*

   Edgar must shake off his _____________, and tolerate him, at least.
   a. petulance
   b. obeisance
   c. solicitude
   d. antipathy

Classic Grammar • Parts of Speech

Every vocabulary word is a part of speech, and every sentence is made of vocabulary. To use vocabulary correctly, we must use it grammatically. Many words can be used in several ways.

In the sentences below, you will find our classic vocabulary words, but they may be present as a different part of speech. In other words, you may see a classic adjective we know but in its adverb form or noun form. Think flexibly. On the lines below sentences three through seven, write the part of speech of each word.

1.   Almost   every   night   some   pencil   marks   were   **effaced**. (Melville)
    adv.   adj.   n.   adj.   adj.   n.   v.   v.

2.   He was **voluble** like a youngster on the eve of a long holiday. (Conrad)
    pron. v.   adj.   prep. adj.   n.   prep. adj. n. prep.adj. adj.   n.

3.   No   entreaties   will   move   the   **obdurate**   Hassan. (Thackeray)
    adj.   n.   v.   v.   adj.   adj.   n.

4.   I was chiefly **edified**, I am afraid, by the pictures.... (Dickens)
    pron. v.   adv.   v.   pron. v.   adj.   prep. adj.   n.

5.   The **transient** fears of the company were now forgotten. (Eliot)
    adj.   adj.   n. prep. adj.   n.   v.   adv.   v.

6.   He threw back her suggestions with a restless **petulance**. (Stowe)
    pron.   v.   adv. adj.   n.   prep. adj. adj.   n.

7.   He made his **obeisance** before the throne of King Harold. (Scott)
    pron.   v.   adj.   n.   prep.   adj.   n.   prep. ---------n.----------

Classic Word Muddles

In most of the sentences below, one of the classic words is misused, which means that it is a part of speech error. Can you explain the vocabulary/grammar errors? Some of the sentences contain no errors.

1. For him, the statement was an important **edify**.   not a n.
2. He began to **antipathy** the sound of the bird.   *antipathy* is a n.
3. The complication was a **ruminate** problem.   not an adj.
4. His **obdurate** refusal to cooperate angered everyone.   correct
5. The cause of the collapse was completely **ascertain**.   not an adj.
6. The tedious man was a complete **voluble**.   not a n.
7. It is not polite to **epithet** someone.   not a v.
8. He comforted them with sincere **solicitude**.   correct
9. The attendant made a subtle **obeisance** gesture.   not an adj.
10. Suddenly a stranger **accosted** my uncle, begging for money.   correct

Classic Centuries: *ruminate*

Below are examples of how *ruminate* has been used through the centuries. Which is your favorite?

1955   Joseph Heller, *Catch-22*
    "He rested a moment in critical rumination."
1946   Robert Penn Warren, *All the King's Men*
    "The boss ruminatively turned the glass in his hand."
1891   Herman Melville, *Billy Budd*
    "Billy found him off duty in a dog watch ruminating by himself."
1886   Robert Louis Stevenson, *Dr. Jekyll and Mr. Hyde*
    "Utterson ruminated awhile."
1878   Thomas Hardy, *The Return of the Native*
    "While he ruminated, a footstep descended the stairs."
1851   Herman Melville, *Moby Dick*
    "Much might be ruminated here, concerning the essential dignity of this regal process."
1623   William Shakespeare, *Othello*
    "I prithee speak to me as to thy thinkings, as thou dost ruminate."

An Impression, Influenced by George Eliot's *Silas Marner*

In the story below, most of the classic words are used well, but one is not. It may be the meaning that is wrong, or it may be the grammar/usage. Please circle the classic word that is not used correctly.

In the early years of this century, there was a humble linen-weaver in the village of Raveloe who wove his linen every day, ruminating over the somber questions of his life. Silas Marner, for that was his name, was a small, sallow, aging figure at the edge of society. No one really knew him, though people spoke volubly of him as though they did. His life was meager; he had no superfluous resources. When neighbors passed by, Silas made a small but courteous obeisance, but he obdurately declined to participate in the events of the village, and this failure of congeniality generated a touch of antipathy among the affronted villagers. Neighborhood boys furtively crept close to his stone cottage to peek at him, afraid to accost him directly. They feared that he was a malevolent creature, a petulant or even cruel eccentric, and from time to time Silas would stand up from his loom and throw open the door, casting a reproving eye their way. The boys would scatter and flee, fearing for their lives.

In his silent and solitary sufficiency, Silas was not despondent or melancholy. He had his work, and though he did not feel benevolence from the villagers, he also did not feel their enmity. He did not feel obsequious toward them. He was content to sit at his loom assiduously, working during the light of the day, confident that his good work would in time edify the villagers as to his value to the community.

Even this small expectation was a false hope, for it is ever the habit of neighbors to grimace at the wrongs of others, to interpret misunderstood actions as malevolent, and to be quicker to reprove than to accept. Silas's neighbors were discomfited by his tacit contentment. They spoke of him with derision. They mistrusted his quiet satisfaction, judging him as complacent and malevolent. They described him in **epithet** language. They regarded him not as amiable or polite but as an odious eccentric, and the more listless and indolent they were themselves, the more suspicious they were of his indefatigable labor. Why could he not be jovial and join in the social events of the village? What grotesque secret was he hiding? In their profound sagacity, they found it convenient to judge Silas, to ridicule his physiognomy, and to characterize his pensive manner as bitter and misanthropic.

Classic Words Character

Let us use some of the words that we are learning. Pretend that you are writing a novel, and write a short description of a character, using some of the words in this lesson. Here is an example:

> Many of her friendships had been transient. This was different. In this friendship she could ascertain the elements of lifelong solicitude, and she found herself remonstrating inwardly against her fears that it would not last. She had a stolid confidence that she and Fido would be pals forever.

Classic Words Place

Now write a short description of a place, a landscape, or a scene, using some of the words in this lesson. Here is an example:

> He disliked the noisy, voluble clamor of the place, the customers filling the air with their petulance and their obdurate hostility to anyone different from themselves, remonstrating pointlessly against every real individual. Livid epithets roared above the noise, and superfluous insults flew across the room. It was difficult to ascertain the point of all this antipathy.

Classic Words Invention

Finally, write a short description of something or someone that you imagine, using some of the words in this lesson. Here is an example:

> The ceremony seemed to her a superfluous obeisance to unremarkable effort. She could not, in her sagacity, see why they were making such an issue of celebrating his accomplishment when all of them did work that was as good or better. She stood with a stolid countenance and watched.

Instructor Section

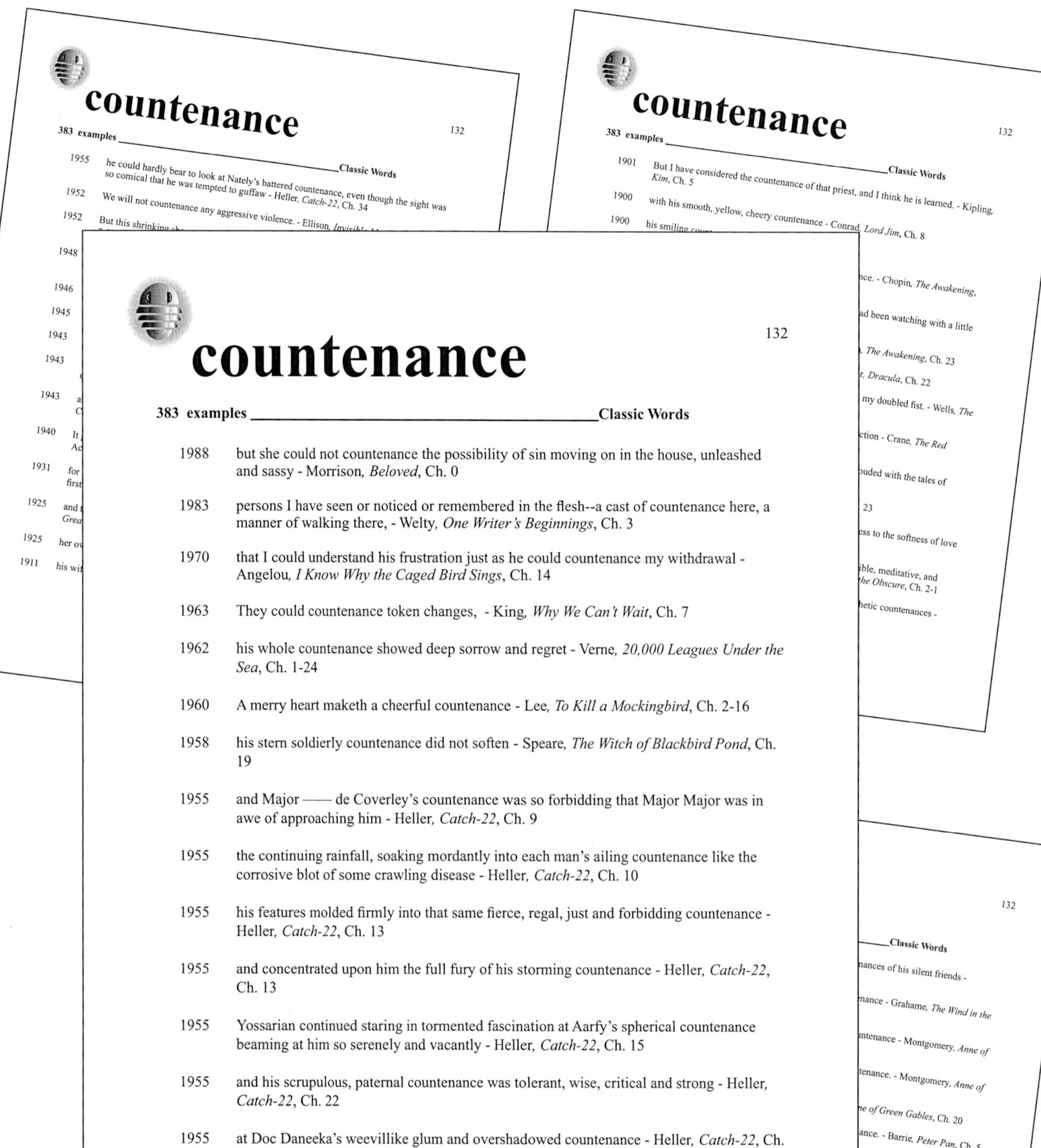

countenance

1988   but she could not countenance the possibility of sin moving on in the house, unleashed and sassy - Morrison, *Beloved*, Ch. 0

1983   persons I have seen or noticed or remembered in the flesh--a cast of countenance here, a manner of walking there, - Welty, *One Writer's Beginnings*, Ch. 3

1970   that I could understand his frustration just as he could countenance my withdrawal - Angelou, *I Know Why the Caged Bird Sings*, Ch. 14

1963   They could countenance token changes, - King, *Why We Can't Wait*, Ch. 7

1962   his whole countenance showed deep sorrow and regret - Verne, *20,000 Leagues Under the Sea*, Ch. 1-24

1960   A merry heart maketh a cheerful countenance - Lee, *To Kill a Mockingbird*, Ch. 2-16

1958   his stern soldierly countenance did not soften - Speare, *The Witch of Blackbird Pond*, Ch. 19

1955   and Major —— de Coverley's countenance was so forbidding that Major Major was in awe of approaching him - Heller, *Catch-22*, Ch. 9

1955   the continuing rainfall, soaking mordantly into each man's ailing countenance like the corrosive blot of some crawling disease - Heller, *Catch-22*, Ch. 10

1955   his features molded firmly into that same fierce, regal, just and forbidding countenance - Heller, *Catch-22*, Ch. 13

1955   and concentrated upon him the full fury of his storming countenance - Heller, *Catch-22*, Ch. 13

1955   Yossarian continued staring in tormented fascination at Aarfy's spherical countenance beaming at him so serenely and vacantly - Heller, *Catch-22*, Ch. 15

1955   and his scrupulous, paternal countenance was tolerant, wise, critical and strong - Heller, *Catch-22*, Ch. 22

1955   at Doc Daneeka's weevillike glum and overshadowed countenance - Heller, *Catch-22*, Ch. 26

---

countenance

383 examples ____Classic Words 132

1955   he could hardly bear to look at Nately's battered countenance, even though the sight was so comical that he was tempted to guffaw - Heller, *Catch-22*, Ch. 34

1952   We will not countenance any aggressive violence. - Ellison, *Invisible...*

1952   But this shrinking sh...

---

countenance

383 examples ____Classic Words 132

1901   But I have considered the countenance of that priest, and I think he is learned. - Kipling, *Kim*, Ch. 5

1900   with his smooth, yellow, cheery countenance - Conrad, *Lord Jim*, Ch. 8

1900   his smiling count...

---

132 — Classic Words

... and cheery countenances were being piloted over, - Conrad, *Heart of Darkness*, Ch. 1

1902   smiles and frowns chasing each other over that open countenance like sunshine and shadow on a wind-swept plain - Conrad, *Heart of Darkness*, Ch. 2

1902   it was not a brutal countenance, but it was prim, hard and stern, with a firm-set, thin-lipped mouth, and a coldly intolerant eye. - Doyle, *The Hound of the Baskervilles*, Ch. 13

1901   His face, by the full ray of the kerosene lamp, changed and darkened, and Kim, used as every beggar must be to watching countenances, took good note. - Kipling, *Kim*, Ch. 2

IMPLEMENTATION

The implementation strategy of this literary vocabulary program is dictated by the importance of the content itself. These are 200 powerful words that must be known. They are a necessary component of an educated vocabulary. A strong reading experience is the essence of advanced education, and the goal for this vocabulary program is to prepare students to read the essential works of British and American literature by installing literary vocabulary ahead of time, just at the critical moment, so that as the students begin to read great literature, they already know the major literary words. They will not have to struggle with the vocabulary and try to enjoy the stories at the same time.

Enthusiasm is a necessary element, both for ourselves and for our students. Students rarely love any educational content more than their instructors do. Enthusiasm is the force that propels teachers into exciting lessons and propels students into a life of reading, long after they have left school. We want the students to love both words and literature, so any shallow method focused on a banal objective of "raising scores" without inculcating a love for the knowledge is to be avoided. We have to keep our eye on the ball: the vocabulary of literature. We cannot allow grading or assessment or points to displace the excitement of literary vocabulary from the students' minds. The program will do its part to raise scores, but that is a minor byproduct of raising reading and raising knowledge, and not the object of focus. If we keep the program exciting and grounded in meaning, that will do more for scores than any tedious points-based program. Advanced education is what we are about.

The words in this text were identified by my Classic Words research. During a period of thirty years, I have compiled a database that examines the vocabulary of dozens of classic British and American novels, and the words in this text are those that the research has demonstrated to be central. I did not decide which words are most important; the research did. On the facing page you see four sheets of examples of *countenance*, arranged by date of publication; the full printout, however, goes for twenty-eight pages—twenty-eight pages of examples of *countenance*. I could present a similar printout for any of the words in this book. So when I say that a word is a classic word, I am not guessing. I know that the word is in all of those books. The literary vocabulary chosen for this text is unique in quality; there is no such thing as a better list. These are the words that are replete in the literature.

200: Ten Lessons of Twenty Words

This program provides ten vocabulary lessons, with each lesson contributing twenty words—ten new words and ten review words brought forward from *Caesar's English I* and *Caesar's English II*—for a total of 200 great literary vocabulary words. These words should be launched early in the curriculum so that they can illuminate the reading of classic literature during the course.

It is in the nature of these words that they are more challenging to internalize than, for example, a Latin stem. We easily learn that *pre* means *before*, and it is almost automatic, but when we learn that a *rebuke* is a kind of criticism, the content is more elusive.

The Myth of THE Definition

The vocabulary challenge is dramatically intensified by the fact that the very idea of a definition—word *x* means exactly definition *y*—is to some extent arbitrary, incomplete, and misleading. Dictionaries are works of scholarly art, not scientific facts. Pick five great dictionaries and look up the same word, and you will find five different presentations. In fact, there is typically not one definition but a number of different meanings that require their own definitions. All of those definitions were written by definition writers, and the definitions in different dictionaries were written by different definition writers. We do confirm substantial agreement in the definitions, but the wordings and details will always be as individual as the scholars who write them.

Accordingly, in a book such as this one, to say that *languor is a weakness* is only shorthand, a way to *begin explaining*. Having said that, we then have to discuss the nuances of meaning that a word such as *languor* can contain. Instead of a simple learning object such as *x* means *y*, we now have a learning object such as *x* means *y* but sometimes *z* and can also mean.... It is complicated.

So what does this mean—the fact that there is no one sacred, true, short, and right definition, or the fact that each word likely has various possible meanings, each one without a single true, universal, right definition?

It means time. It means that we have to relax. It means that we cannot be too Type A. It means that we must slow down, talk about the words, pick favorite examples, and so forth. It means that we have to look at a word one way and then another, and to look at it and then look at it again, and again. We cannot skim or hurry. It is not a race; it is a picnic. Haste kills fun. We have to take the pleasant time to get used to a word. We have to let fun do its job.

Lesson Components

Each lesson has a collection of components, and you are encouraged to fit your instruction to the details of your teaching situation. You may be able to complete all of the activities in each lesson, but you also may need to be more selective and to choose which activities you and your students wish to do. The lessons are designed to be flexible.

Before we examine the lesson components individually, let us look at three properties that all of the lessons have in common. One is that each lesson focuses on a great writer. A second property is that many of the example sentences are actual quotations from famous books, allowing students to see how great writers have used the words we are learning. This will give students confidence and prevent them from thinking that these 200 words are just a random, arbitrary list. There is nothing arbitrary about this list; these are the words that are most prominent in the literature. The third property of every lesson is a strong emphasis on the grammar of the vocabulary. Grammar is the key to usage. Every word is a part of speech, and vocabulary is grammar in action.

Nearly all of the lessons begin with a photograph of a writer, and on the facing page is the list of twenty words featured in the lesson.

Classic Words – Lesson I

Ten New Words

latter: the second	**aloof**: unfriendly
dejected: in low spirits	**dissipate**: disperse
despondent: disheartened	**portent**: an omen
rebuke: a sharp criticism	**phenomenon**: an unusual occurrence
writhe: twist, squirm	**resolute**: determined

Ten Review Words

Caesar's English I	*Caesar's English II*
countenance: facial expression	**placate**: to appease
profound: deep	**derision**: ridicule
manifest: obvious	**vivacious**: full of life
prodigious: huge	**procure**: to acquire
languor: weakness	**retort**: a quick, clever reply

12   13

The list presents ten new words at the top and ten review words below, five brought forward from *Caesar's English I* and five from *Caesar's English II*. The definitions beside the words are the initial shorthand of meaning, and we will use those brief definitions for quizzes, but on the very next page we move into the greater complexity of real meaning that attends each of the words.

---

latter: adj., LATT-ur, rhymes with *bladder*

The adjective **latter** means the second item of two. If there are more than two items, we simply refer to the "last mentioned." In *The Red Badge of Courage*, Stephen Crane wrote that "The latter felt immensely superior to his friend." In Emily Bronte's *Wuthering Heights*, we read that "She tossed a cushion under his head, and offered him some water; he rejected the latter, and tossed uneasily on the former."

dejected: adj., de-JECK-ted, rhymes with *collected*

The adjective **dejected** means sad or depressed, as the stems *de* (down) and *ject* (throw) suggest: thrown down, emotionally. The noun form is *dejection*. In James M. Barrie's *Peter Pan*, we read that "Hook was profoundly dejected." In Sir Walter Scott's *Ivanhoe*, Scott noted that "Her demeanour was serious, but not dejected."

despondent: adj., de-SPON-dent, rhymes with *correspondent*

The adjective **despondent** (the noun forms are *despondence, despond,* or *despondency*) means profoundly disheartened, dispirited from loss of hope. In Kenneth Grahame's *The Wind in the Willows*, we read that "He's always rather low and despondent when he's wanting his victuals." Victuals are food. In *Gulliver's Travels*, Jonathan Swift wrote that "I found myself so listless and desponding that I had not the heart to rise."

rebuke: n. or v., re-BYOOK, rhymes with *fluke*

The noun **rebuke** indicates a sharp reprimand, a severe criticism. We also use *rebuke* as a verb. In Charles Dickens's *A Tale of Two Cities*, we read that "Loud acclamations hailed this rebuke." In William Makepeace Thackeray's *Vanity Fair*, "That gentleman rose up with an oath and rebuked Rawdon for his language."

writhe: v., RYTHE, rhymes with *scythe*

The verb **writhe** means to twist or to squirm, to contort the body. In Thomas Hardy's *Jude the Obscure*, we read that "Sue writhed under the hard and direct questioning." In Mary Shelley's *Frankenstein*, the pitiful monster laments, "I now writhed under the miserable pain of a wound."

14

aloof: adj., ah-LOOF, rhymes with *roof*

The adjective **aloof** means distant, unfriendly, cool. It is often used with *stand*; we stand aloof, either emotionally or physically. In Jane Austen's *Pride and Prejudice*, "They stood a little aloof while he was talking to their niece." James M. Barrie, in *Peter Pan*, wrote, "Ever a dark and solitary enigma, he stood aloof from his followers."

dissipate: v., DISS-ih-pate, rhymes with *anticipate*

The verb **dissipate** means to disperse, to scatter, to break up, to disappear. The noun *dissipation* usually refers to an undisciplined life of luxury or pleasure. In Mary Shelley's *Frankenstein*, we read that "Presently a breeze dissipated the cloud, and I descended upon the glacier." In *Walden*, Henry David Thoreau wrote that "The student may read Homer or Aeschylus in the Greek without danger of dissipation or luxuriousness."

portent: n., POR-tent, rhymes with *important*

The noun **portent** means an omen, a warning sign. The adjective form is *portentous*. In *Lord Jim*, Joseph Conrad wrote that "They had him, but it was like getting hold of an apparition, a wraith, a portent." In Herman Melville's *Moby Dick*, we read that "Such a portentous and mysterious monster roused all my curiosity."

phenomenon: n., feh-NOH-me-non, rhymes with *Parthenon*

The singular noun **phenomenon** refers to a fact or situation that may not be fully understood. Important: The plural is *phenomena*: a phenomenon, some phenomena. In *The Yearling*, Marjorie Kinnan Rawlings wrote that "The sinkhole was a phenomenon common to the Florida limestone regions." In Henry David Thoreau's *Walden*, we read that "Few phenomena gave me more delight."

resolute: adj., REH-zo-loot, rhymes with *salute*

The adjective **resolute** means determined or firm, usually in an admirable sense. The opposite is *irresolute*. In Bram Stoker's *Dracula*, we read that "He was never so resolute, never so strong, never so full of volcanic energy, as at present."

15

In this two-page spread you will find each of the ten new words examined in some detail. Let us zoom in on one example from Lesson I so that we can see what it contains.

---

despondent: adj., de-SPON-dent, rhymes with *correspondent*

The adjective **despondent** (the noun forms are *despondence, despond,* or *despondency*) means profoundly disheartened, dispirited from loss of hope. In Kenneth Grahame's *The Wind in the Willows*, we read that "He's always rather low and despondent when he's wanting his victuals." Victuals are food. In *Gulliver's Travels*, Jonathan Swift wrote that "I found myself so listless and desponding that I had not the heart to rise."

Each listing presents the word, the typical grammar usage, a pronunciation guide, and a rhyme, though sometimes the rhymes are only approximate. Following that is a short explanation of the meaning, which goes beyond the shorthand definition on the first page of the chapter. Sometimes other part of speech forms are presented; in the case of the adjective *despondent*, we also see the noun forms of *despondence*, *despond*, and *despondency*. Finally, we see examples of the word in sentences by famous authors; these have the merit not only of showing students wonderful examples but also of patiently immersing students in the names of the authors and the titles of the classics. These sentences give students motivating proof that the words really do matter. When the students finally read those books, they will have heard of them many times and will know that they are famous.

The ten new words get this special treatment, but the ten review words do not. I have already presented the review words in detail in the *Caesar's English* books, and students who did not read those books will have little disadvantage because there are myriad examples of review word sentences throughout this book.

What should you do with these pages? I would read over them together, one listing at a time. Read the definition, look at the alternative parts of speech, say the rhyme aloud, and examine the examples, deciding which one you like best. This will take some time. Good. Time teaches. When you finish the first five, talk about which of the five is most interesting, or new, or most likely to be useful, and so forth. Then do the same thing when you finish discussing the next five.

Following the pages of close-ups, each lesson contains a reading and then a poem on facing pages. The purpose of the reading is to accustom students to the feeling of nonfiction, while also increasing their exposure to the words of the lesson. This reading is a bit unrealistic in that all of these great literary words are more common in fiction, but it is still worthwhile to soak in the facts and the tone of nonfiction, where contractions and first person are not appropriate. The most important part of this activity, then, is reading itself. Students should read the page to themselves, perhaps more than once, and then think about the question at the bottom before discussing it with you. We do not want the reading to be followed by a quiz or worksheet of any kind. The reading experience is half of the activity, and the discussion with you is the other half.

Jack London
The ability to read academic nonfiction is one of the most important elements of academic success. For practice, here is a short nonfiction essay that contains many of the classic words of this lesson.

A writer of rugged **countenance** and **prodigious** talent, Jack London was the author of *White Fang*, *The Call of the Wild*, *The Sea Wolf*, and other stories that have become classics of American literature.

Born in San Francisco in 1876, London knew from an early age that he wanted to be a writer, but he spent years struggling **despondently** from one low-paying job to another. He worked at a cannery, was an oyster-pirate, worked on the California Fish Patrol, was a sailor, and was even a hobo—in 1894 the **dejected** London was incarcerated for thirty days for vagrancy. Eventually he returned home, graduated from Oakland High School, and was admitted to the University of California at Berkeley, but he dropped out because he did not have enough money to pay his university bills. London was a great reader, and in his later years he **procured** a personal library of more than 15,000 books.

In 1897 London went to the Alaskan Klondike, **resolutely** chasing a dream of gold, but he suffered under the cruel conditions and developed scurvy. His experiences left him with a **profound** social conscience, and he began to weave his experiences into **vivacious** stories that depicted the struggle for existence amid the cruel **phenomena** of wild nature, where the weak and **languorous** are dominated by the strong. He wrote his first major novel, *The Call of the Wild*, which is set in the Yukon, in 1903. *The Call of the Wild* has never been out of print since it was first published, and it has now been translated into nearly fifty languages.

All authors experience sharp critical reviews, even **derision**, and London was no different. Some have questioned his **manifest** emphasis on violence, and others have **rebuked** him for ethnocentric prejudice. It is not unusual for writers to draw on other sources for ideas, but some critics feel that London went beyond normal influence and plagiarized other authors' work—a charge he rejected.

Since London's death in 1916 at the age of only forty, his fame as a novelist has not **dissipated**. His major titles are part of the canon of world literature, and they continue to be read and discussed.

Q: What interests you most about Jack London's life? What would you like to read more about?

16

Jack London
Michael Clay Thompson

Jack London stumbled down the dock.
Dejection hurt his heart.   n.
An omen had appeared, a flock.
a **portent**, dark, a start   n.

of some **phenomenon**. He looked   n.
into the **writing** wind,   adj.
his canvas backpack crammed with books,
and dreamed of spinning

tales of cold, **despondent** worlds,   adj.
of snow, **prodigious** storms,   adj.
and brutes, **rebukes**, and whirling   n.
mists with **dissipating** forms   adj.

of circling wolves. A **languor** filled   n.
his listless limbs. He stowed
his stuff aboard the ship. He'd build
these grimy details into code,

into his art of words, **aloof**.   adj.
of Nature's fallen fools,
of ice and knives, and fang and tooth,
and **countenances** cruel.   n.

He well perceived the **portent's** truth: n.
the **resolute** survive.   n.
The weak succumb to fang and tooth,
the strong prevail—alive.

17

The poem on the facing page is important in a number of ways. It typically mimics the feature author's work. It also accustoms students to the genre of poetry. It shows the vocabulary in context, and it offers, if you choose to do it, an option for students to determine the part of speech of the words in bold. They are not in bold in the student edition, nor do the answers that appear at right show in the student edition.

One aspect of this activity should be noted: You will sometimes see a word such as *writhing*, which looks like a verb, identified as an adjective. This is because the word is not acting as a verb; it is a verbal use, with *writhing* modifying a noun: *the writhing wind*. Students who have never studied verbals before will be challenged by this, and it would be unfair to make this a graded exercise, assigning points for correct identifications of parts of speech. Instead, this is an open discussion that allows you to talk about why a word such as *writhing* might be an adjective in a sentence. As you keep finding such usages, they will lose their strangeness and feel normal. Part of what this means is that our grammar instruction must include verbals: gerunds, participles, and infinitives.

To work the poem page, therefore, you might do something like this: First read the poem silently. Then read the poem aloud. Then ask the students to find all of the classic words that are in the poem, which is easy to do because in your instructor manual the words are in black against the other words in gray. Then discuss the poem's tone or meaning or theme. Finally, go down the line of classic words, deciding what part of speech each one is in the context of its sentence. The more you do that, the more students will think of vocabulary in terms of grammar. Vocabulary and grammar are two aspects of the same thing.

After the poem, the lesson provides a Classic Words Challenge, followed by a parts of speech challenge.

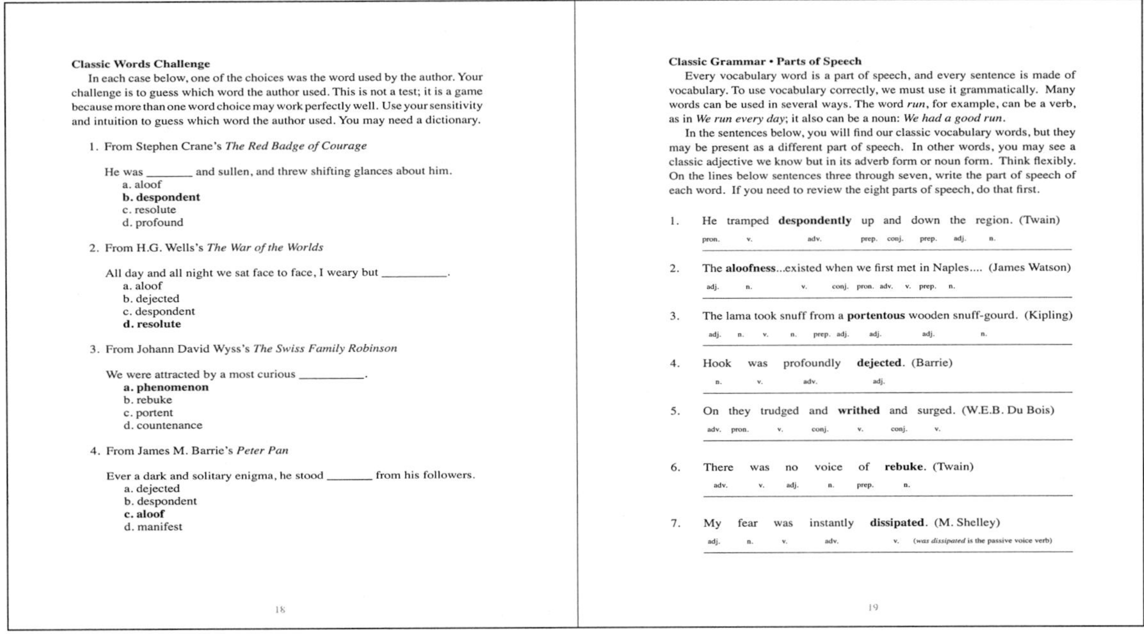

Classic Words Challenge

In each case below, one of the choices was the word used by the author. Your challenge is to guess which word the author used. This is not a test; it is a game because more than one word choice may work perfectly well. Use your sensitivity and intuition to guess which word the author used. You may need a dictionary.

1. From Stephen Crane's *The Red Badge of Courage*

   He was _______ and sullen, and threw shifting glances about him.
   a. aloof
   b. despondent
   c. resolute
   d. profound

2. From H.G. Wells's *The War of the Worlds*

   All day and all night we sat face to face, I weary but _______.
   a. aloof
   b. dejected
   c. despondent
   d. resolute

3. From Johann David Wyss's *The Swiss Family Robinson*

   We were attracted by a most curious _______.
   a. phenomenon
   b. rebuke
   c. portent
   d. countenance

4. From James M. Barrie's *Peter Pan*

   Ever a dark and solitary enigma, he stood _______ from his followers.
   a. dejected
   b. despondent
   c. aloof
   d. manifest

18

Classic Grammar • Parts of Speech

Every vocabulary word is a part of speech, and every sentence is made of vocabulary. To use vocabulary correctly, we must use it grammatically. Many words can be used in several ways. The word *run*, for example, can be a verb, as in *We run every day*; it also can be a noun: *We had a good run*.

In the sentences below, you will find our classic vocabulary words, but they may be present as a different part of speech. In other words, you may see a classic adjective we know but in its adverb form or noun form. Think flexibly. On the lines below sentences three through seven, write the part of speech of each word. If you need to review the eight parts of speech, do that first.

1. He tramped **despondently** up and down the region. (Twain)
   pron.   v.   adv.   prep.   conj.   prep.   adj.   n.

2. The **aloofness**...existed when we first met in Naples.... (James Watson)
   adj.   n.   v.   conj.   pron.   adv.   v.   prep.   n.

3. The lama took snuff from a **portentous** wooden snuff-gourd. (Kipling)
   adj.   n.   v.   n.   prep.   adj.   adj.   adj.   n.

4. Hook was profoundly **dejected**. (Barrie)
   n.   v.   adv.   adj.

5. On they trudged and **writhed** and surged. (W.E.B. Du Bois)
   adv.   pron.   v.   conj.   v.   conj.   v.

6. There was no voice of **rebuke**. (Twain)
   adv.   v.   adj.   n.   prep.   n.

7. My fear was instantly **dissipated**. (M. Shelley)
   adj.   n.   v.   adv.   v.   (*was dissipated* is the passive voice verb)

19

The classic word challenge is not a graded quiz but a thought problem. There are four sentences from famous authors, each containing one of our classic words. The problem is: Which word did the author actually use? This activity works well as a student-to-student discussion in which the students go through the options and guess which of the words the author used. Once the students make their guesses, then you can use this manual to discuss the answers.

> 1. From Stephen Crane's *The Red Badge of Courage*
>
> He was _______ and sullen, and threw shifting glances about him.
> a. aloof
> **b. despondent**
> c. resolute
> d. profound

The parts of speech activity is what in my grammar programs I call a one-level analysis.

---

4.   Hook   was   profoundly   **dejected**. (Barrie)

    n.   v.   adv.   adj.

5.   On   they   trudged   and   **writhed**   and   surged. (W.E.B. Du Bois)

    adv.   pron.   v.   conj.   v.   conj.   v.

There are seven sentences, with the first two worked out as models. For the next five sentences, students are asked to identify the part of speech of every word in the sentence, including the classic word that appears there. To the right of the sentence is the name of the author who wrote the sentence. This assumes a certain grammar background in order to discuss the reasons for the identifications, but a knowledge of the eight parts of speech is a reasonable expectation at this level. The point of this activity is to further strengthen vocabulary usage as a function of grammar. Grammar and usage are one.

On the following page spread, there are three activities: Muddles, Centuries, and an Impression.

Classic Word Muddles

In most of the sentences below, one of the classic words is misused, which means that it is a part of speech error. Remember, parts of speech are the instructions for correct vocabulary usage. Can you explain the vocabulary/grammar errors? Some of the sentences contain no errors.

1. When Austen saw the **writhe**, she became more resolute.   not a n.
2. His dejection increased, and he made a **countenance** face.   not an adj.
3. The **rebuke** remark made Hawthorne stand aloof.   not an adj.
4. The latter remark caused **portent** alarm.   not an adj.
5. The disturbing portent left London **despondent**.   correct
6. Thoreau thought about a prodigious **phenomena**.   phenomenon
7. Crane's dejected countenance made his sadness **manifest**.   correct
8. Dickinson's sleepy languor gave her a manifest **aloof**.   not a n.
9. Frost chose the latter path, and his dejection **dissipated**.   correct
10. The comment stung, and he made a **writhe** face.   not an adj.

Classic Centuries: *dejected*

Below are examples of how *dejected* has been used through the centuries. Which is your favorite?

1952   Bernard Malamud, *The Natural*
        "The New York Yankees grew more dejected."
1904   James M. Barrie, *Peter Pan*
        "He was roused from this dejection by Smee's eager voice."
1895   Stephen Crane, *The Red Badge of Courage*
        "Their smudged countenances now expressed a profound dejection."
1816   Jane Austen, *Emma*
        "His dejection was most evident."
1726   Jonathan Swift, *Gulliver's Travels*
        "They all appeared with dejected looks, and in the meanest habit."
1667   John Milton, *Paradise Lost*
        "Of sorrow and dejection and despair...."
1601   William Shakespeare, *Hamlet*
        "Nor the dejected 'havior of the visage."

An Impression, Influenced by Jack London's *The Sea Wolf*

In the story below, some of the classic words are used well, but others are not. Sometimes it is the meaning that is wrong, and other times it is the grammar/usage. Please circle the classic words that are not used correctly.

The scarred old captain clanked across the wooden deck of the schooner, muttering sharp rebukes at his crew. His usual cheerful **dejection** was gone, and he seemed to writhe in fury at his failure to find the pirates that had attacked his ship during the last voyage. He might have been negligent, or he might have been tricked; he preferred the latter explanation. But now he was in no mood for reflection. Aloof and glowering, he stomped past the nervous crew.

In fact, he was in no mood for hesitation; he was furious, energetic, and **languorous**, and he was resolute about catching the pirates. He would allow no retort. He knew that it might take a **phenomenon** event to reveal where they were hiding, and he knew that the answer might be hidden and **manifest**. The situation could be a **profound**.

He remembered the days of his youth, when he had been so hopeful and **despondent**, but those hopes had rapidly dissipated as a series of disturbing portents had proven true. Instead of realizing his dreams, he had suffered under years of **prodigious**, and he knew that now it was too late for him to recover. His only hope was to find the pirates and exact his revenge. Nothing could placate him.

Purple and gray clouds began to amass on the southern horizon, and he knew that a prodigious storm was gathering and **dissipating.** Flocks of birds were flying north high over the mast quickly, as though they were frightened. A swooping seagull dropped a snake from the sky, and it landed on the salty deck, writhing and hissing, and he knew that this was a portent of danger, a disturbing **phenomena.** Far at sea, you had to watch the weather closely. He barked out a command to set the course for north-northwest.

On a small island far to the west, the pirates could just see the captain's sails on the horizon like a white speck of foam on the crest of a wave, and they knew that he was sailing away from them, and they laughed in **dejection**.

The Muddles are messes. The activity contains ten sentences, in most of which a classic word is misused. The catch is that in one or more sentences, the usage is correct. Students are asked to examine each sentence and determine if the usage is correct or not. In this manual I have provided hints that indicate the reason a usage is wrong, and I have indicated which sentences are correct.

The Classic Centuries activity gives students a chronological series of example sentences for a classic word, in some cases going back centuries. Seeing how long ago the earliest usage was gives students a sense of time and motivational evidence for the importance of the word during the history of British and American literature.

The Impression is a fun piece that mimics the feature author's work in style and in content. It gives students an opportunity for reading, but there is a catch. In each piece, one or more of the classic words is an error, either of meaning or of grammar, and the students are asked to find the problem(s). This is another activity designed to amplify students' awareness of vocabulary as a function of grammar.

The final activity in each lesson is a series of three short writing assignments. You might ask students to do all three, but it would also be good to ask them to pick one of the assignments to do. The task is to use the classic words to write a passage of fiction, such as a description of a character, a setting, a scene, or something else that we might find in a novel.

Classic Words Character

Let us use some of the words that we are learning. Pretend that you are writing a novel, and write a short description of a character, using some of the words in this lesson. Here is an example:

Madeline's countenance was disturbed. The rebuke from her mother had left her writhing with disappointment, and now she felt the sting of the derision in her mother's words. She knew that the pain of hurt feelings would eventually dissipate, and her mother might even come to her room and try to placate her resentment, but for now, all she wanted to do was sit in a corner and think of a sharp retort.

Classic Words Place

Now write a short description of a place, a landscape, or a scene, using some of the words in this lesson. Here is an example:

During the storm, the birch trees had writhed in profound submission to the wind, and the dark clouds had frowned their derisive countenances down upon the valley. The storm was a massive phenomenon, somehow aloof from humanity and yet resolute in bringing life-giving water to the fields. Now, the first hint of vivacious sun began to break through the clouds, and the thunder began to dissipate, but only slowly.

Classic Words Invention

Finally, write a short description of something or someone that you imagine, using some of the words in this lesson. Here is an example:

Freedom is a profound idea. Life without freedom is a kind of despondence, a prodigious suppression of creativity and individuality, but freedom is also a challenging phenomenon because with freedom we become responsible for rising above languor and accomplishing something meaningful in our lives.

22

Quizzes and Review Tests

Following the activities of each lesson, there is a quiz, which is not contained in the student book. This manual contains ten lesson quizzes that may be copied and given to students. It also contains answer keys. Each regular quiz contains twenty-five items divided into five sections. Here are the instructions for the five sections, with one example question for each one:

Please write the classic word that best replaces what is bold.
1.   His **facial expression** was sad and dejected. ___________________

Please define the classic word in bold.
6.   The **aloof** stranger did not return my friendly greeting.___________

For each word in bold, please write the abbreviation of its part of speech.
11. His **despondence** increased as the light began to fade. ___________

For each sentence, circle the classic word that best completes the sentence.
16. The snake (writhed, rebuked) on the ground.

Please circle the best antonym (opposite) of the classic word in bold.
21. **dejected**: sad, deep, huge, vivacious

As you can see, the quizzes are learning experiences that go beyond typical memorization to make the students think.

In addition to the ten regular lesson quizzes, there are two review tests: one covering Lessons I through V, and the other covering Lessons I through X. These review tests each contain fifty items. At the top of the review test, there are thirty items that ask the students to define the classic word, and at the bottom of the test, there are twenty items that ask the student to provide the classic word, given the definition. It is important to have students process the literary vocabulary both ways, from word to definition and from definition to word.

An Implementation Schedule: Two Weeks Per Lesson

It is important to launch the vocabulary program early so that it is coming into place as the literature appears. If we list the components of each lesson, this is what we get:

<u>Lesson Overview</u>
1. Photo of Feature Author
2. List of 20 Classic Words
3. Expanded Discussion of the Classic Words
4. Biographical Article in Nonfiction Style
5. Mimic Poem
6. Classic Words Challenge
7. Classic Grammar: Parts of Speech
8. Classic Word Muddles
9. Classic Centuries
10. An Impression
11. Three Classic Words Paragraph Problems
12. Lesson Quiz

Some of these, such as the photo, the biographical article, the centuries, or the impression, should not be time-consuming. It will be an easy task to do two activities in one session. You can remain flexible about which and how many activities you do. If an activity seems to require more time than you had allotted, that is fine. To rush it in order to force-fit it to your schedule risks damaging the feeling of the activity. We want to present every activity in a way that is enthusiastic and motivational.

It is possible to move through this book at a pace of one lesson per week, and if we allow a week for each review test, that comprises a twelve-week plan. That pace, however, would require a substantial amount of time per week—even per day—and would most likely not be beneficial to the students because the pace may overwhelm them. If we set the pace too fast, any content becomes overwhelming.

A better plan is a two-week plan. During the first week, we would introduce the list, practice the words and definitions, and do a few activities at an enjoyable pace. We might do some memory practice on Monday, Wednesday, and Friday and an activity or two on Tuesday and Thursday. On the second week of the lesson, we would continue to do a bit of memory work, complete the remaining activities, and then conclude the week on Friday with the quiz, after which we would devote a few minutes to introducing the vocabulary of the next lesson.

A rough schedule could look something like this:

	Mon	Tues	Weds	Thurs	Fri
Wk 1	drill	activities	drill	activities	drill
Wk 2	activities	drill	activities	drill	quiz

View this flexibly. In actual practice each session will probably combine both some drill and an activity, the difference being a matter of emphasis. By *drill* I mean studying the initial list page and then the two-page expanded discussion of the words that follows. We want students to become thoroughly familiar with the words and the contents of those three pages. Go back to those pages repeatedly until the students have absorbed them.

That pace would occupy twenty weeks, and if we add a week for each review test, we would have a twenty-two week program. A pace like that allows for flexibility. We would be able to devote an extra week to shore up the vocabulary if necessary, and we could even skip a week or two if we were in the middle of a great novel. With a dash of flexibility, this vocabulary program will last six months or so. After that, every classic that the students read will continue to reinforce the words that they have studied here.

Ideally, the vocabulary and literature programs would operate simultaneously. It might be good to give the vocabulary a few weeks to build up before launching the literature, but the two elements are mutually reinforcing; as students read almost any British or American classic—*Treasure Island*, for example—they will see the vocabulary appearing before their eyes.

Quizzes

Words Lesson I Quiz

Please write the classic word that best replaces what is bold.
1. His **facial expression** was sad and dejected.______________________
2. A **deep** languor spread through the dog's limbs.______________________
3. The wounded creature **squirmed** and whimpered. ______________________
4. The strange **omen** worried the prospector. ______________________
5. The **harsh criticism** irritated the inspector. ______________________

Please define the classic word in bold.
6. The **aloof** stranger did not return my friendly greeting. ______________
7. A weary **languor** filled his exhausted limbs.______________________
8. The **latter** choice seemed more advantageous.______________________
9. Gradually, the fog began to **dissipate**.______________________
10. The challenge was daunting, but he was **resolute**. ______________________

For each word in bold, please write the abbreviation of its part of speech.
11. His **despondence** increased as the light began to fade.______________
12. A strange, glowing **phenomenon** began to brighten the sky. __________
13. The **prodigious** storm blanketed the Klondike with snow.__________
14. By the next morning, his **dejection** had begun to abate.____________
15. His countenance clearly **manifested** his derision. ______________

For each sentence, circle the classic word that best completes the sentence.
16. The snake (writhed, rebuked) on the ground.
17. Finally, the reason for his anger became (manifest, dejected).
18. Of the two solutions, we preferred the (retort, latter).
19. The displeased owner severely (rebuked, manifested) the fellow.
20. Aldrich was more than dejected; he was (resolute, despondent).

Please circle the best antonym (opposite) of the classic word in bold.
21. **dejected**: sad, deep, huge, vivacious
22. **manifest**: obvious, subtle, depressed, friendly
23. **profound**: shallow, disheartened, close, small
24. **aloof**: dejected, strong, amiable, resolute
25. **rebuke**: poem, insult, observation, praise

Classic Words Lesson I Quiz Answer Key

Please write the classic word that best replaces what is bold.
1. His **facial expression** was sad and dejected.   countenance
2. A **deep** languor spread through the dog's limbs.   profound
3. The wounded creature **squirmed** and whimpered.   writhed
4. The strange **omen** worried the prospector.   portent
5. The **harsh criticism** irritated the inspector.   rebuke

Please define the classic word in bold.
6. The **aloof** stranger did not return my friendly greeting.   unfriendly
7. A weary **languor** filled his exhausted limbs.   weakness
8. The **latter** choice seemed more advantageous.   second
9. Gradually, the fog began to **dissipate**.   disperse
10. The challenge was daunting, but he was **resolute**.   determined

For each word in bold, please write the abbreviation of its part of speech.
11. His **despondence** increased as the light began to fade.   n.
12. A strange, glowing **phenomenon** began to brighten the sky.   n.
13. The **prodigious** storm blanketed the Klondike with snow.   adj.
14. By the next morning, his **dejection** had begun to abate.   n.
15. His countenance clearly **manifested** his derision.   v.

For each sentence, circle the classic word that best completes the sentence.
16. The snake (**writhed**, rebuked) on the ground.
17. Finally, the reason for his anger became (**manifest**, dejected).
18. Of the two solutions, we preferred the (retort, **latter**).
19. The displeased owner severely (**rebuked**, manifested) the fellow.
20. Aldrich was more than dejected; he was (resolute, **despondent**).

Please circle the best antonym (opposite) of the classic word in bold.
21. **dejected**: sad, deep, huge, **vivacious**
22. **manifest**: obvious, **subtle**, depressed, friendly
23. **profound**: **shallow**, disheartened, close, small
24. **aloof**: dejected, strong, **amiable**, resolute
25. **rebuke**: poem, insult, observation, **praise**

Classic Words Lesson II Quiz

Please write the classic word that best replaces what is bold.
1. A great **wave** of anger surged over him. ______________________________
2. His **friendly** manner put everyone at ease. ______________________________
3. He **earnestly begged** her to reconsider her decision. ______________________
4. She was **embarrassed** by the cruel things she had said.______________________
5. The strange remark left him **confused** and worried.______________________

Please define the classic word in bold.
6. There were **myriad** reasons for his resentment. ______________________
7. A brooding **melancholy** oppressed his mood.______________________
8. The **plaintive** cry of the owl pierced the night.______________________
9. He tried to **conjure** forth the memory of his father. ______________________
10. His plan was based only on **conjecture**, not on facts.______________________

For each word in bold, please write the abbreviation of its part of speech.
11. The **singular** situation made everyone ill at ease.______________________
12. He felt no **fervor** for the task but did it dutifully. ______________________
13. The sharp and undeserved **reproof** annoyed the family.______________________
14. "I would **fain** do the work myself," he replied.______________________
15. She worked with a **serene** spirit to tend to her mother.______________________

For each sentence, circle the classic word that best completes the sentence.
16. She (entreated, perplexed) him for an explanation.
17. He tried to (entreat, conjure) stories to tell his daughter.
18. He was overwhelmed by the (myriads, billows) of options.
19. She was saddened by the (prostrate, plaintive) cries of the loon.
20. The (serenity, fervor) of the calm, blue sky restored her mood.

Please circle the best antonym (opposite) of the classic word in bold.
21. **fervor**: interest, enthusiasm, indifference, hobby
22. **plaintive**: cheerful, audible, abashed, singular
23. **amiable**: cheerful, agreeable, aloof, benevolent
24. **reprove**: criticize, dissipate, conjure, applaud
25. **serene**: still, fervent, peaceful, profuse

Classic Words Lesson II Quiz Answer Key

Please write the classic word that best replaces what is bold.
1. A great **wave** of anger surged over him.   billow
2. His **friendly** manner put everyone at ease.   amiable
3. He **earnestly begged** her to reconsider her decision.   entreated
4. She was **embarrassed** by the cruel things she had said.   abashed
5. The strange remark left him **confused** and worried.   perplexed

Please define the classic word in bold.
6. There were **myriad** reasons for his resentment.   countless
7. A brooding **melancholy** oppressed his mood.   sadness
8. The **plaintive** cry of the owl pierced the night.   mournful
9. He tried to **conjure** forth the memory of his father.   summon
10. His plan was based only on **conjecture**, not on facts.   guess

For each word in bold, please write the abbreviation of its part of speech.
11. The **singular** situation made everyone ill at ease.   adj.
12. He felt no **fervor** for the task but did it dutifully.   n.
13. The sharp and undeserved **reproof** annoyed the family.   n.
14. "I would **fain** do the work myself," he replied.   adv.
15. She worked with a **serene** spirit to tend to her mother.   adj.

For each sentence, circle the classic word that best completes the sentence.
16. She (**entreated**, perplexed) him for an explanation.
17. He tried to (entreat, **conjure**) stories to tell his daughter.
18. He was overwhelmed by the (**myriads**, billows) of options.
19. She was saddened by the (prostrate, **plaintive**) cries of the loon.
20. The (**serenity**, fervor) of the calm, blue sky restored her mood.

Please circle the best antonym (opposite) of the classic word in bold.
21. **fervor**: interest, enthusiasm, **indifference**, hobby
22. **plaintive**: **cheerful**, audible, abashed, singular
23. **amiable**: cheerful, agreeable, **aloof**, benevolent
24. **reprove**: criticize, dissipate, conjure, **applaud**
25. **serene**: still, **fervent**, peaceful, profuse

Classic Words Lesson III Quiz

Please write the classic word that best replaces what is bold.
1. His face was a **sickly yellow** color. _______________________
2. She made a **sharp facial expression** at his mistake._______________
3. They were **cheerful** as they reached the summit. _______________
4. He was **sullen** and resentful about the event. _______________
5. There was a weird, **distorted** face looking in the window._____________

Please define the classic word in bold.
6. Her **droll** sense of humor delighted him. _______________
7. His self-assurance had abated into a **diffidence.**_______________
8. He **winced** at the very thought. _______________
9. She was **listless** and exhausted for weeks. _______________
10. He gracefully **alluded** to his mistake. _______________

For each word in bold, please write the abbreviation of its part of speech.
11. The **condescending** reply offended them._______________
12. He **entreated** her to reconsider his request. _______________
13. **Exquisite** ironwork adorned the front doorway._______________
14. He sank into **morose** and dejected spirits._______________
15. She smiled **diffidently** and replied, "I think not."_______________

For each sentence, circle the classic word that best completes the sentence.
16. He (winced, evinced) at the distasteful suggestion.
17. The young fellow was shy, introverted, and (jovial, diffident).
18. During her long illness she had a(n) (sallow, acute) countenance.
19. His guilt was (manifest, plaintive) on his doleful countenance.
20. He had given up, as his (amiable, despondent) expression revealed.

Please circle the best antonym (opposite) of the classic word in bold.
21. **jovial**: cheerful, morose, droll, ostentatious
22. **acute**: dull, profound, droll, doleful
23. **wince**: evince, reprove, smile, wink
24. **diffidence**: shyness, confidence, fervor, serenity
25. **confound**: perplex, clarify, evince, rebuke

Classic Words Lesson III Quiz Answer Key

Please write the classic word that best replaces what is bold.
1. His face was a **sickly yellow** color.   sallow
2. She made a **sharp facial expression** at his mistake.   grimace
3. They were **cheerful** as they reached the summit.   jovial
4. He was **sullen** and resentful about the event.   morose
5. There was a weird, **distorted** face looking in the window.   grotesque

Please define the classic word in bold.
6. Her **droll** sense of humor delighted him.   amusing
7. His self-assurance had abated into a **diffidence**.   lack of confidence
8. He **winced** at the very thought.   shrank involuntarily
9. She was **listless** and exhausted for weeks.   uninterested
10. He gracefully **alluded** to his mistake.   indirectly referred to

For each word in bold, please write the abbreviation of its part of speech.
11. The **condescending** reply offended them.   adj.
12. He **entreated** her to reconsider his request.   v.
13. **Exquisite** ironwork adorned the front doorway.   adj.
14. He sank into **morose** and dejected spirits.   adj.
15. She smiled **diffidently** and replied, "I think not."   adv.

For each sentence, circle the classic word that best completes the sentence.
16. He (**winced**, evinced) at the distasteful suggestion.
17. The young fellow was shy, introverted, and (jovial, **diffident**).
18. During her long illness she had a(n) (**sallow**, acute) countenance.
19. His guilt was (**manifest**, plaintive) on his doleful countenance.
20. He had given up, as his (amiable, **despondent**) expression revealed.

Please circle the best antonym (opposite) of the classic word in bold.
21. **jovial**: cheerful, **morose**, droll, ostentatious
22. **acute**: **dull**, profound, droll, doleful
23. **wince**: evince, reprove, **smile**, wink
24. **diffidence**: shyness, **confidence**, fervor, serenity
25. **confound**: perplex, **clarify**, evince, rebuke

Classic Words Lesson IV Quiz

Please write the classic word that best replaces what is bold.
1. There were small **swirls** of smoke in the sky. _______________________
2. As the battle began, there was a horrible **racket** of gunfire. _______________
3. He was sick, and his countenance was **pallid**. _______________________
4. She issued a stern **prohibition** against the practice. _______________________
5. Everyone was careful not to violate **proper behavior**. _______________

Please define the classic word in bold.
6. They were **vexed** by his refusal to cooperate. _______________________
7. She **expostulated** with him about his decision. _______________________
8. He was a bit **incredulous** at her pensive story. _______________________
9. She **venerated** her magnanimous grandfather. _______________________
10. The crowd **clamored** for revenge. _______________________

For each word in bold, please write the abbreviation of its part of speech.
11. He cried out in a sudden **expostulation**. _______________________
12. The clever **expedient** succeeded, and the plan went forward. _________
13. Her **wan** countenance evinced her worsening illness. _______________
14. The **placid** surface of the lake concealed what lurked beneath. _________
15. He **deprecated** the arguments that justified cruelty. _______________

For each sentence, circle the classic word that best completes the sentence.
16. The (din, eddy) hurt his ears.
17. We (venerated, deprecated) his immoral conduct.
18. The enemy troops (clamored, importuned) in anger.
19. She was very shy, even (demure, oblique).
20. Her command was a formal (expedient, injunction).

Please circle the best antonym (opposite) of the classic word in bold.
21. **serene**: pensive, wan, chaotic, placid
22. **decorum**: barbarism, fervor, melancholy, despondence
23. **deprecate**: rebuke, reproach, celebrate, indicate
24. **reproach**: compliment, rebuke, deprecate, importune
25. **vex**: perplex, irritate, please, confuse

Classic Words Lesson IV Quiz Answer Key

Please write the classic word that best replaces what is bold.
1. There were small **swirls** of smoke in the sky.   eddies
2. As the battle began, there was a horrible **racket** of gunfire.   din
3. He was sick, and his countenance was **pallid**.   wan
4. She issued a stern **prohibition** against the practice.   injunction
5. Everyone was careful not to violate **proper behavior**.   decorum

Please define the classic word in bold.
6. They were **vexed** by his refusal to cooperate.   irritated
7. She **expostulated** with him about his decision.   objected earnestly
8. He was a bit **incredulous** at her pensive story.   skeptical
9. She **venerated** her magnanimous grandfather.   respected
10. The crowd **clamored** for revenge.   cried out

For each word in bold, please write the abbreviation of its part of speech.
11. He cried out in a sudden **expostulation**.   n.
12. The clever **expedient** succeeded, and the plan went forward.   n.
13. Her **wan** countenance evinced her worsening illness.   adj.
14. The **placid** surface of the lake concealed what lurked beneath.   adj.
15. He **deprecated** the arguments that justified cruelty.   v.

For each sentence, circle the classic word that best completes the sentence.
16. The (**din**, eddy) hurt his ears.
17. We (venerated, **deprecated**) his immoral conduct.
18. The enemy troops (**clamored**, importuned) in anger.
19. She was very shy, even (**demure**, oblique).
20. Her command was a formal (expedient, **injunction**).

Please circle the best antonym (opposite) of the classic word in bold.
21. **serene**: pensive, wan, **chaotic**, placid
22. **decorum**: **barbarism**, fervor, melancholy, despondence
23. **deprecate**: rebuke, reproach, **celebrate**, indicate
24. **reproach**: **compliment**, rebuke, deprecate, importune
25. **vex**: perplex, irritate, **please**, confuse

Classic Words Lesson V Quiz

Please write the classic word that best replaces what is bold.
1. I **pretended** an indifference that I did not feel.__________________
2. The affable governor replied with a **warlike** bellow. ________________
3. I had **until now** not expressed my objection. __________________
4. It was my **habit** to take a walk every morning.__________________
5. Please go ahead, and I will catch up with you **shortly**.______________

Please define the classic word in bold.
6. The tragic event **affected** my feelings about them.________________
7. He **interposed** a brief rebuke of her assertion. ________________
8. Her **eloquence** made her a popular advocate.________________
9. By dawn the storm had begun to **abate**. __________________
10. The **sublime** ideal appealed to his spirit.__________________

For each word in bold, please write the abbreviation of its part of speech.
11. The wind sent a **tremulous** motion through the leaves. ______________
12. I **vividly** remember the house where I grew up. ________________
13. I had no clear **apprehension** of the reason I was thus rebuked. ________
14. My anonymous **benefactor** left money on my doorstep. ____________
15. My **complacent** assumptions proved to be unfounded. ____________

For each sentence, circle the classic word that best completes the sentence.
16. My heart beat with a (torpid, tremulous) flutter.
17. All attempts have (hitherto, anon) been unsuccessful.
18. Your (eloquent, complacent) words mortified me at last.
19. I must (abate, interpose) a small comment in this discussion.
20. I feel no real (apprehension, complacence) about accepting.

Please circle the best antonym (opposite) of the classic word in bold.
21. **apprehension**: understanding, delirium, perplexity, eloquence
22. **martial**: commanding, affable, vivid, sublime
23. **hitherto**: afterward, exquisite, anon, profound
24. **abate**: recede, worsen, grimace, dissipate
25. **vivid**: sublime, tremulous, eloquent, wan

Classic Words Lesson V Quiz Answer Key

Please write the classic word that best replaces what is bold.
1.   I **pretended** an indifference that I did not feel.   feigned
2.   The affable governor replied with a **warlike** bellow.   martial
3.   I had **until now** not expressed my objection.   hitherto
4.   It was my **habit** to take a walk every morning.   wont
5.   Please go ahead, and I will catch up with you **shortly**.   anon

Please define the classic word in bold.
6.   The tragic event **affected** my feelings about them.   influenced
7.   He **interposed** a brief rebuke of her assertion.   inserted (put between)
8.   Her **eloquence** made her a popular advocate.   effective language
9.   By dawn the storm had begun to **abate**.   lessen
10. The **sublime** ideal appealed to his spirit.   lofty

For each word in bold, please write the abbreviation of its part of speech.
11. The wind sent a **tremulous** motion through the leaves.   adj.
12. I **vividly** remember the house where I grew up.   adv.
13. I had no clear **apprehension** of the reason I was thus rebuked.   n.
14. My anonymous **benefactor** left money on my doorstep.   n.
15. My **complacent** assumptions proved to be unfounded.   adj.

For each sentence, circle the classic word that best completes the sentence.
16. My heart beat with a (torpid, **tremulous**) flutter.
17. All attempts have (**hitherto**, anon) been unsuccessful.
18. Your (**eloquent**, complacent) words mortified me at last.
19. I must (abate, **interpose**) a small comment in this discussion.
20. I feel no real (**apprehension**, complacence) about accepting.

Please circle the best antonym (opposite) of the classic word in bold.
21. **apprehension**: understanding, delirium, **perplexity**, eloquence
22. **martial**: commanding, **affable**, vivid, sublime
23. **hitherto**: **afterward**, exquisite, anon, profound
24. **abate**: recede, **worsen**, grimace, dissipate
25. **vivid**: sublime, tremulous, eloquent, **wan**

Classic Words Review Test, Lessons I through V

Write the definition:

1. manifest _____________________
2. aloof _____________________
3. myriad _____________________
4. prodigious _____________________
5. prostrate _____________________
6. rebuke _____________________
7. hitherto _____________________
8. din _____________________
9. indolent _____________________
10. billow _____________________
11. grimace _____________________
12. sallow _____________________
13. martial _____________________
14. torpid _____________________
15. inexorable _____________________
16. countenance _____________________
17. wince _____________________
18. decorum _____________________
19. placid _____________________
20. feign _____________________
21. doleful _____________________
22. listless _____________________
23. manifest _____________________
24. portent _____________________
25. languor _____________________
26. derision _____________________
27. grotesque _____________________
28. retort _____________________
29. dissipate _____________________
30. abate _____________________

Write the classic word:

31. to acquire _____________________
32. deep _____________________
33. pleased _____________________
34. eagerness _____________________
35. showy _____________________
36. a swirl or whirlpool _____________________
37. to pester _____________________
38. quivering _____________________
39. a guess _____________________
40. unspoken _____________________
41. to appease _____________________
42. confuse _____________________
43. indirect or slanting _____________________
44. lack of confidence _____________________
45. indirectly refer to _____________________
46. generous _____________________
47. to respect _____________________
48. shortly _____________________
49. habit _____________________
50. to deplore _____________________

Classic Words Review Test, Lessons I through V, Answer Key

Write the definition:

1. manifest *obvious*
2. aloof *unfriendly*
3. myriad *countless*
4. prodigious *huge*
5. prostrate *lying flat*
6. rebuke *a sharp criticism*
7. hitherto *until now*
8. din *a racket*
9. indolent *lazy*
10. billow *a wave*
11. grimace *a sharp expression*
12. sallow *sickly yellow*
13. martial *warlike*
14. torpid *sluggish*
15. inexorable *inevitable*
16. countenance *facial expression*
17. wince *to shrink involuntarily*
18. decorum *proper behavior*
19. placid *calm*
20. feign *pretend*
21. doleful *mournful*
22. listless *uninterested*
23. manifest *obvious*
24. portent *an omen*
25. languor *weakness*
26. derision *ridicule*
27. grotesque *distorted*
28. retort *a quick, clever reply*
29. dissipate *disperse*
30. abate *to lessen*

Write the classic word:

31. to acquire *procure*
32. deep *profound*
33. pleased *fain*
34. eagerness *alacrity*
35. showy *ostentatious*
36. a swirl or whirlpool *eddy*
37. to pester *importune*
38. quivering *tremulous*
39. a guess *conjecture*
40. unspoken *tacit*
41. to appease *placate*
42. confuse *perplex*
43. indirect or slanting *oblique*
44. lack of confidence *diffidence*
45. indirectly refer to *allude*
46. generous *magnanimous*
47. to respect *venerate*
48. shortly *anon*
49. habit *wont*
50. to deplore *deprecate*

Classic Words Lesson VI Quiz

Please write the classic word that best replaces what is bold.
1. I stood there, awkward and **uneasy**. _______________________
2. The parent had to **come between** in the dispute._______________
3. His **hateful** prejudice showed his ignorance. _________________
4. I **gestured** wildly in my opposition to the idea. _______________
5. The discussion of the proposal was **lively**. _________________

Please define the classic word in bold.
6. His appearance was wild, **haggard**, and wan._________________
7. Some new crisis was certainly **impending**. __________________
8. The argument had a **plausible** persuasiveness._________________
9. She was **fastidious** in her mathematical precision._____________
10. The new boss imposed **obtrusive** and odious inspections.________

For each word in bold, please write the abbreviation of its part of speech.
11. His **obsequious** apologies irritated them both. _______________
12. The generous **patron** supported the theater. _________________
13. The memories left him in a **wistful** and pensive mood. _________
14. The strict policy **obtruded** into the team's morale. ____________
15. She spoke **animatedly** about the problems of the decision. _______

For each sentence, circle the classic word that best completes the sentence.
16. She wished he were more (fastidious, complacent) about his work.
17. We could not tell how he felt from his (animated, impassive) expression.
18. His denial was (impending, plausible).
19. The theft left him in (ignominy, acquiescence) for years.
20. When he was rescued, he looked (subtle, haggard) and worried.

Please circle the best antonym (opposite) of the classic word in bold.
21. **plausible**: likely, expedient, ridiculous, animated
22. **obsequious**: arrogant, placid, haggard, subtle
23. **intervene**: gesticulate, mortify, interpose, ignore
24. **fastidious**: sage, sloppy, impassive, impending
25. **animated**: ignominious, languorous, plausible, vulgar

Classic Words Lesson VI Quiz Answer Key

Please write the classic word that best replaces what is bold.
1. I stood there, awkward and **uneasy**.   discomfited
2. The parent had to **come between** in the dispute.   intervene
3. His **hateful** prejudice showed his ignorance.   odious
4. I **gestured** wildly in my opposition to the idea.   gesticulated
5. The discussion of the proposal was **lively**.   animated

Please define the classic word in bold.
6. His appearance was wild, **haggard**, and wan.   looking exhausted
7. Some new crisis was certainly **impending**.   about to happen
8. The argument had a **plausible** persuasiveness.   believable
9. She was **fastidious** in her mathematical precision.   detailed
10. The new boss imposed **obtrusive** and odious inspections. intrusive

For each word in bold, please write the abbreviation of its part of speech.
11. His **obsequious** apologies irritated them both.   adj.
12. The generous **patron** supported the theater.   n.
13. The memories left him in a **wistful** and pensive mood.   adj.
14. The strict policy **obtruded** into the team's morale.   v.
15. She spoke **animatedly** about the problems of the decision. adv.

For each sentence, circle the classic word that best completes the sentence.
16. She wished he were more (**fastidious**, complacent) about his work.
17. We could not tell how he felt from his (animated, **impassive**) expression.
18. His denial was (impending, **plausible**).
19. The theft left him in (**ignominy**, acquiescence) for years.
20. When he was rescued, he looked (subtle, **haggard**) and worried.

Please circle the best antonym (opposite) of the classic word in bold.
21. **plausible**: likely, expedient, **ridiculous**, animated
22. **obsequious**: **arrogant**, placid, haggard, subtle
23. **intervene**: gesticulate, mortify, interpose, **ignore**
24. **fastidious**: sage, **sloppy**, impassive, impending
25. **animated**: ignominious, **languorous**, plausible, vulgar

Classic Words Lesson VII Quiz

Please write the classic word that best replaces what is bold.
1.   We had a delightful **visit** in Naples. _________________________
2.   The eerie **specter** rose up before us in the night. _______________
3.   I resisted **attributing** malicious intentions to him._______________
4.   It was a **touching** parting that saddened everyone._______________
5.   She began to **think deeply** about the concept. _________________

Please define the classic word in bold.
6.   The **orthodox** view is more widely accepted._________________
7.   The room was **austere**, with only a mattress on the floor. _________
8.   The explanation was wild and barely **intelligible**. ______________
9.   The dictator **oppressed** the people mercilessly. ________________
10. His **ardor** was unabated, even after a year._________________

For each word in bold, please write the abbreviation of its part of speech.
11. Time did not **mitigate** the suffering in her heart. ________________
12. We remained for a **fortnight**, discussing every option. ___________
13. His **genial** personality concealed his resentment. ______________
14. Your answer was **equivocal**; what do you really mean?_____________
15. The **furtive** movement in the trees caught his eye.______________

For each sentence, circle the classic word that best completes the sentence.
16. His language was expressive and (articulate, furtive).
17. The tyrant was cruel and (meditative, oppressive).
18. His views were very traditional, even (profane, orthodox).
19. The bare surroundings were more (austere, poignant) than mine.
20. We hid in the thick (tumult, verdure) of the forest.

Please circle the best antonym (opposite) of the classic word in bold.
21. **poignant**: cheerful, sad, boring, profane
22. **ardor**: enthusiasm, passion, indifference, oppression
23. **orthodox**: serious, trendy, intelligible, genial
24. **verdure**: sojourn, ardor, apparition, desert
25. **intelligible**: perplexing, clear, magnanimous, profane

Classic Words Lesson VII Quiz Answer Key

Please write the classic word that best replaces what is bold.
1.   We had a delightful **visit** in Naples.   sojourn
2.   The eerie **specter** rose up before us in the night.   apparition
3.   I resisted **attributing** malicious intentions to him.   imputing
4.   It was a **touching** parting that saddened everyone.   poignant
5.   She began to **think deeply** about the concept.   meditate

Please define the classic word in bold.
6.   The **orthodox** view is more widely accepted.   traditional
7.   The room was **austere**, with only a mattress on the floor.   bare
8.   The explanation was wild and barely **intelligible**.   understandable
9.   The dictator **oppressed** the people mercilessly.   tyrannized
10. His **ardor** was unabated, even after a year.   enthusiasm, passion

For each word in bold, please write the abbreviation of its part of speech.
11. Time did not **mitigate** the suffering in her heart.   v.
12. We remained for a **fortnight**, discussing every option.   n.
13. His **genial** personality concealed his resentment.   adj.
14. Your answer was **equivocal**; what do you really mean?   adj.
15. The **furtive** movement in the trees caught his eye.   adj.

For each sentence, circle the classic word that best completes the sentence.
16. His language was expressive and (**articulate**, furtive).
17. The tyrant was cruel and (meditative, **oppressive**).
18. His views were very traditional, even (profane, **orthodox**).
19. The bare surroundings were more (**austere**, poignant) than mine.
20. We hid in the thick (tumult, **verdure**) of the forest.

Please circle the best antonym (opposite) of the classic word in bold.
21. **poignant**: **cheerful**, sad, boring, profane
22. **ardor**: enthusiasm, passion, **indifference**, oppression
23. **orthodox**: serious, **trendy**, intelligible, genial
24. **verdure**: sojourn, ardor, apparition, **desert**
25. **intelligible**: **perplexing**, clear, magnanimous, profane

Classic Words Lesson VIII Quiz

Please write the classic word that best replaces what is bold.
1.   He had a superficial **appearance** of innocence. _______________________
2.   She wrote **diligently** long into the night._______________________
3.   He entertained the group with **short accounts** of his life. ____________
4.   They intended to **repay** him for his strong support. _______________
5.   There was a **touchable** sense of fear in the room. _______________

Please define the classic word in bold.
6.   Her **indefatigable** effort paid off handsomely. _______________
7.   His rugged **physiognomy** was widely admired. _______________
8.   The deed set an **irrevocable** process in motion. _______________
9.   The **congenial** friend shared many of his interests. _______________
10. She sank slowly into an **abyss** of despair._______________

For each word in bold, please write the abbreviation of its part of speech.
11. There was a certain unhealthy **pallor** in his countenance. ____________
12. A purple light **suffused** the morning sky. _______________
13. He uttered an **incongruous** laugh at the tragic news. _______________
14. His **pertinacity** defied all attempts to change his opinion._______________
15. She had a **congenial** disposition to be interested in everyone. _________

For each sentence, circle the classic word that best completes the sentence.
16. The great news brought true (felicity, malevolence) to the group.
17. The dissatisfaction soon (requited, pervaded) the army.
18. He succeeded because of his (congenial, assiduous) hard work.
19. Her (indefatigable, ambiguous) effort impressed her boss.
20. We were struck by her elegant (physiognomy, malevolence).

Please circle the best antonym (opposite) of the classic word in bold.
21. **assiduous**: negligent, pertinacious, congenial, irrevocable
22. **ambiguous**: congenial, clear, pallid, irrevocable
23. **pallid**: rosy, suffused, malevolent, palpable
24. **felicity**: delight, malevolence, despondence, physiognomy
25. **incongruous**: harmonic, malevolent, assiduous, palpable

Classic Words Lesson VIII Quiz Answer Key

Please write the classic word that best replaces what is bold.
1. He had a superficial **appearance** of innocence.   semblance
2. She wrote **diligently** long into the night.   assiduously
3. He entertained the group with **short accounts** of his life.   anecdotes
4. They intended to **repay** him for his strong support.   requite
5. There was a **touchable** sense of fear in the room.   palpable

Please define the classic word in bold.
6. Her **indefatigable** effort paid off handsomely.   tireless
7. His rugged **physiognomy** was widely admired.   facial features
8. The deed set an **irrevocable** process in motion.   unalterable
9. The **congenial** friend shared many of his interests.   agreeable
10. She sank slowly into an **abyss** of despair.   bottomless depth

For each word in bold, please write the abbreviation of its part of speech.
11. There was a certain unhealthy **pallor** in his countenance.   n.
12. A purple light **suffused** the morning sky.   v.
13. He uttered an **incongruous** laugh at the tragic news.   adj.
14. His **pertinacity** defied all attempts to change his opinion.   n.
15. She had a **congenial** disposition to be interested in everyone. adj.

For each sentence, circle the classic word that best completes the sentence.
16. The great news brought true (**felicity**, malevolence) to the group.
17. The dissatisfaction soon (requited, **pervaded**) the army.
18. He succeeded because of his (congenial, **assiduous**) hard work.
19. Her (**indefatigable**, ambiguous) effort impressed her boss.
20. We were struck by her elegant (**physiognomy**, malevolence).

Please circle the best antonym (opposite) of the classic word in bold.
21. **assiduous: negligent**, pertinacious, congenial, irrevocable
22. **ambiguous**: congenial, **clear**, pallid, irrevocable
23. **pallid: rosy**, suffused, malevolent, palpable
24. **felicity**: delight, malevolence, **despondence**, physiognomy
25. **incongruous: harmonic**, malevolent, assiduous, palpable

Classic Words Lesson IX Quiz

Please write the classic word that best replaces what is bold.
1. There is no **trace** of the civilization that lived here. ___________________
2. In an **outpouring** of remorse, he begged forgiveness. ________________
3. The remark was an **insult** to his years of dedication. ________________
4. We need to **list** the items that must be packed. ________________
5. He had an **unconventional** attitude about the issue.________________

Please define the classic word in bold.
6. He attempted to **traverse** the cliff face. ___________________
7. The policy was an **impediment** to his plan. ___________________
8. The **luminous** chemical had a blue glow. ___________________
9. He was **disconsolate** and cried out pitifully.___________________
10. Her **imperious** manner offended everyone. ___________________

For each word in bold, please write the abbreviation of its part of speech.
11. There were **sundry** benefits to the new plan. ________________
12. The substance was **opaque**, and we could not see through it. __________
13. I felt a sudden **enmity** for the villains who had done this. ____________
14. There was no **tangible** reward to be gained.________________
15. The remark was an **affront** to my reputation.________________

For each sentence, circle the classic word that best completes the sentence.
16. We began to (enumerate, affront) the many reasons.
17. I was furious, and my (effusion, enmity) only increased later.
18. We found no remains, no (impediment, vestige) of the settlement.
19. The (luminous, effusive) glow of the reaction lit the sky.
20. The regulation was a serious (censure, impediment) to our plan.

Please circle the best antonym (opposite) of the classic word in bold.
21. **affront**: effusion, compliment, enumeration, repose
22. **disconsolate**: malevolent, indefatigable, sanguine, fastidious
23. **imperious**: humble, proud, angry, assiduous
24. **enmity**: complacence, diffidence, eloquence, friendship
25. **impediment**: effusion, enumeration, assistance, censure

Classic Words Lesson IX Quiz Answer Key

Please write the classic word that best replaces what is bold.
1. There is no **trace** of the civilization that lived here.   vestige
2. In an **outpouring** of remorse, he begged forgiveness.   effusion
3. The remark was an **insult** to his years of dedication.   affront
4. We need to **list** the items that must be packed.   enumerate
5. He had an **unconventional** attitude about the issue.   eccentric

Please define the classic word in bold.
6. He attempted to **traverse** the cliff face.   cross
7. The policy was an **impediment** to his plan.   obstruction
8. The **luminous** chemical had a blue glow.   light-emitting
9. He was **disconsolate** and cried out pitifully.   inconsolable
10. Her **imperious** manner offended everyone.   overbearing

For each word in bold, please write the abbreviation of its part of speech.
11. There were **sundry** benefits to the new plan.   adj.
12. The substance was **opaque**, and we could not see through it.   adj.
13. I felt a sudden **enmity** for the villains who had done this.   n.
14. There was no **tangible** reward to be gained.   adj.
15. The remark was an **affront** to my reputation.   n.

For each sentence, circle the classic word that best completes the sentence.
16. We began to (**enumerate**, affront) the many reasons.
17. I was furious, and my (effusion, **enmity**) only increased later.
18. We found no remains, no (impediment, **vestige**) of the settlement.
19. The (**luminous**, effusive) glow of the reaction lit the sky.
20. The regulation was a serious (censure, **impediment**) to our plan.

Please circle the best antonym (opposite) of the classic word in bold.
21. **affront**: effusion, **compliment**, enumeration, repose
22. **disconsolate**: malevolent, indefatigable, **sanguine**, fastidious
23. **imperious**: **humble**, proud, angry, assiduous
24. **enmity**: complacence, diffidence, eloquence, **friendship**
25. **impediment**: effusion, enumeration, **assistance**, censure

Classic Words Lesson X Quiz

Please write the classic word that best replaces what is bold.
1. We attempted to **make sure** what the reason was. ___________________
2. He was a **bad-tempered** and malevolent grouch.___________________
3. We had hoped that the example would **instruct** him. ________________
4. She began to **think deeply** about the lunar eclipse. ________________
5. I appreciated her **concern** for the child's feelings. ________________

Please define the classic word in bold.
6. We gradually conceived an **antipathy** for the event. ________________
7. He was a tedious and **voluble** individual. ________________
8. The sunset cast a **transient** glow in the west.________________
9. He tried to **efface** her image from his memory.________________
10. She was **obdurate** in her stance on the issue.________________

For each word in bold, please write the abbreviation of its part of speech.
11. His history lecture **edified** the audience.________________
12. After his **obdurate** refusal, the group ignored him. ________________
13. The queen was famous for her political **sagacity**.________________
14. He was **prostrate** on the ground, not supine. ________________
15. She slowly **ascertained** the cause of the earthquake. ________________

For each sentence, circle the classic word that best completes the sentence.
16. We had to (ruminate, remonstrate) carefully before speaking.
17. She gave good advice because of her (sagacity, antipathy).
18. They (ascertained, effaced) all trace of the graffiti from the wall.
19. His (petulant, transient) attitude irritated everyone.
20. Their (voluble, stolid) and unemotional faces made us hesitate.

Please circle the best antonym (opposite) of the classic word in bold.
21. **petulant**: obdurate, transient, voluble, congenial
22. **stolid**: animated, torpid, odious, haggard
23. **obeisance**: solicitude, sagacity, affront, felicity
24. **edified**: livid, perplexed, voluble, petulant
25. **transient**: voluble, stolid, chronic, livid

Classic Words Lesson X Quiz Answer Key

Please write the classic word that best replaces what is bold.
1. We attempted to **make sure** what the reason was.   ascertain
2. He was a **bad-tempered** and malevolent grouch.   petulant
3. We had hoped that the example would **instruct** him.   edify
4. She began to **think deeply** about the lunar eclipse.   ruminate
5. I appreciated her **concern** for the child's feelings.   solicitude

Please define the classic word in bold.
6. We gradually conceived an **antipathy** for the event.   deep dislike
7. He was a tedious and **voluble** individual.   speaking incessantly
8. The sunset cast a **transient** glow in the west.   brief
9. He tried to **efface** her image from his memory.   erase
10. She was **obdurate** in her stance on the issue.   refusing to change

For each word in bold, please write the abbreviation of its part of speech.
11. His history lecture **edified** the audience.   v.
12. After his **obdurate** refusal, the group ignored him.   adj.
13. The queen was famous for her political **sagacity**.   n.
14. He was **prostrate** on the ground, not supine.   adj.
15. She slowly **ascertained** the cause of the earthquake.   v.

For each sentence, circle the classic word that best completes the sentence.
16. We had to (**ruminate**, remonstrate) carefully before speaking.
17. She gave good advice because of her (**sagacity**, antipathy).
18. They (ascertained, **effaced**) all trace of the graffiti from the wall.
19. His (**petulant**, transient) attitude irritated everyone.
20. Their (voluble, **stolid**) and unemotional faces made us hesitate.

Please circle the best antonym (opposite) of the classic word in bold.
21. **petulant**: obdurate, transient, voluble, **congenial**
22. **stolid**: **animated**, torpid, odious, haggard
23. **obeisance**: solicitude, sagacity, **affront**, felicity
24. **edified**: livid, **perplexed**, voluble, petulant
25. **transient**: voluble, stolid, **chronic**, livid

Classic Words Review Test, Lessons I through X

Write the definition:

1. luminous _______________
2. affront _______________
3. acquiescence _______________
4. requite _______________
5. vex _______________
6. ascertain _______________
7. semblance _______________
8. malevolence _______________
9. latter _______________
10. efface _______________
11. genial _______________
12. entreat _______________
13. odious _______________
14. sundry _______________
15. jovial _______________
16. expedient _______________
17. discomfit _______________
18. indefatigable _______________
19. resolute _______________
20. sagacity _______________
21. sublime _______________
22. abashed _______________
23. tedious _______________
24. effusion _______________
25. ruminate _______________
26. interpose _______________
27. palpable _______________
28. verdure _______________
29. sojourn _______________
30. enmity _______________

Write the classic word:

31. to instruct _______________
32. sluggish _______________
33. spread throughout _______________
34. bruised or pale _______________
35. a trace _______________
36. believable _______________
37. attribute to _______________
38. alleviate _______________
39. miserable _______________
40. bare _______________
41. touching, sad _______________
42. bad-tempered _______________
43. cringing, submissive _______________
44. lying flat _______________
45. a gesture of respect _______________
46. a two-week period _______________
47. without emotion _______________
48. diligent _______________
49. sullen _______________
50. deep dislike _______________

Classic Words Review Test, Lessons I through X, Answer Key

Write the definition:

1. luminous *light-emitting*
2. affront *an insult*
3. acquiescence *passive compliance*
4. requite *to repay*
5. vex *to irritate*
6. ascertain *to make sure*
7. semblance *appearance*
8. malevolence *ill will*
9. latter *the second*
10. efface *erase*
11. genial *kind*
12. entreat *ask earnestly*
13. odious *hateful*
14. sundry *various*
15. jovial *cheerful*
16. expedient *a convenient means*
17. discomfit *to make uneasy*
18. indefatigable *tireless*
19. resolute *determined*
20. sagacity *wisdom*
21. sublime *lofty*
22. abashed *embarrassed*
23. tedious *boring*
24. effusion *an outpouring*
25. ruminate *think deeply*
26. interpose *put between*
27. palpable *touchable*
28. verdure *vegetation*
29. sojourn *a visit*
30. enmity *hostility*

Write the classic word:

31. to instruct *edify*
32. sluggish *torpid*
33. spread throughout *pervade*
34. bruised or pale *livid*
35. a trace *vestige*
36. believable *plausible*
37. attribute to *impute*
38. alleviate *mitigate*
39. miserable *abject*
40. bare *austere*
41. touching, sad *poignant*
42. bad-tempered *petulant*
43. cringing, submissive *obsequious*
44. lying flat *prostrate*
45. a gesture of respect *obeisance*
46. a two-week period *fortnight*
47. without emotion *impassive*
48. diligent *assiduous*
49. sullen *morose*
50. deep dislike *antipathy*